THE ★★★★★ UNCLE SAM

Activity Book

★ ★ ★ ★ ★ ★ ★ ★

Language Development Handouts to Teach U.S. History and Government

Carolyn Bohlman
Catherine Porter

CONTEMPORARY BOOKS
a division of NTC/CONTEMPORARY PUBLISHING GROUP
Lincolnwood, Illinois USA

ISBN: 0-8092-0491-6

Published by Contemporary Books,

a division of NTC/Contemporary Publishing Group, Inc.

©2000 NTC/Contemporary Publishing Group, Inc.,

4255 West Touhy Avenue, Lincolnwood (Chicago), Illinois 60712-1975 U.S.A.

3 4 5 6 7 8 9 0 VLP VLP 0 5 4 3 2

Contents

Acknowledgments

I want to thank my husband, Dennis, for his enthusiasm and support; my children—Jennifer, Mark, Daniel, and Matthew—for their understanding and cooperation; and my mother, Alice Klos, for her help in countless ways.

C.B.

Many thanks to Anne, for her endless patience; to Mike, for his analysis of the bingo activities; to Christopher, for his report from the Capitol; and to my parents, for their loving encouragement over the years.

C.P.

About This Book

The *Uncle Sam Activity Book* is a collection of reproducible, classroom-ready handouts to develop language skills while teaching U.S. history and government. A wide variety of activities at different levels is included so that teachers may use the materials selectively, choosing activities appropriate for their students' level and needs. The high-interest activities provide

- ★ innovative techniques for literacy, beginning, intermediate, and multilevel classes.

- ★ integrative practice of listening, speaking, reading, and writing skills.

- ★ comprehensive civics content based on the INS questions on U.S. history and government.

- ★ a variety of learning tasks, games, and songs to appeal to different learning styles and multiple intelligences.

- ★ interactive exercises to foster cooperative learning.

Components of *The Uncle Sam Activity Book* include teacher's notes for activities, the activity handouts, and two appendices. A cassette tape to accompany the book is an integral part of the activity program.

Teacher's Notes for Activities

Comprehensive teacher's notes for each activity include information on the following:

Materials. The handouts, *The Uncle Sam Activity Tape*, and classroom supplies needed for the activities are listed.

Type of Activity. Activities are organized as individual, pair, small group, or whole class.

Language Development. The language skill focus of each activity is specified: listening, speaking, reading, or writing. Where applicable, specific reading skills are noted: sight reading, graphical literacy (skills necessary for comprehending maps, charts, and time lines), scanning, sequencing, and predicting.

INS Questions. See Appendix on page 34.

Level. The activities are designed to accommodate the learning styles of a variety of student populations:

Literacy Level—beginning to low-intermediate students who are *nonliterate* in their native language or English (that is, they may have attained some oral fluency in English but have little or no reading and/or writing ability)

Beginning Level—beginning-level students who are *literate* in English

Multilevel—any combination of the above levels

The levels specified for activities are only suggestions; adapt activities as necessary.

About This Book

Directions. Presentation suggestions and step-by-step instructions are given for each activity. When an activity is appropriate for a variety of levels, specific directions are included for each level. Because the handouts lend themselves to a wide variety of activities, you will no doubt find many creative uses for them in addition to those suggested.

Activity Script. Scripts are furnished for the listening activities. You can either read the script aloud or play *The Uncle Sam Activity Tape.* Using the tape is recommended, since it controls the pace and gives students the chance to hear voices other than their teacher's.

Follow-up Activities. A variety of extension activities is suggested to relate content to students' life experiences and to provide integrated skill development.

Activity Handouts

Seventy-six reproducible blackline masters on perforated pages that can be removed easily and photocopied are bound in *The Uncle Sam Activity Book.* The numbers on the handouts correspond to the numbers on the Teacher's Notes for Activities in the front of the book.

Appendices

INS Questions. The activities cover the one hundred questions on U.S. history and government typical of those used at the INS interview for naturalization. The Teacher's Notes for each activity list the INS questions (cross-referenced to Appendix A) both explicitly covered in and closely related to the content of an activity. The list of questions and answers are organized into content categories for ease in review. When possible, the exact wording of INS questions is used in the activities; however, for actual interview practice, reword the questions in a variety of ways.

Because the INS questions provide a basis for general understanding of U.S. history and government content for anyone (not only naturalization applicants), you can use this list for general review in any course that includes civics content.

Song Lyrics. Complete lyrics to the six songs recorded on *The Uncle Sam Activity Tape* are found in Appendix B. Activities based on these songs are found throughout the book.

Cassette Tape

The Uncle Sam Activity Tape contains the six songs and six Activity Scripts given in the book. The tape also contains the one hundred INS questions (including answers) found in Appendix A, the thirty statements from the INS Reading/Writing Test (for dictation practice), and 15 reworded questions that assess students' mastery of the content and provide additional interview practice.

Teacher's Notes for Activities

Units 1-9

Unit 1
Know Your U.S.A.

1 YOUR CIVIC IDENTITY— UNITED STATES MAP

Materials: handout 1

Type of Activity: individual

Language Development: listening, graphical literacy

INS Questions: 95, 96, 97, 98, 99 (see page 38)

Level: literacy, beginning

Directions: Prepare students for this activity by drawing the outline of your state on the chalkboard. Review the names of the state, city, and state capital. Indicate the locations of your city and state capital. Print the names of the state, city, and state capital on the board.

 Distribute copies of handout 1. Have students find their state and trace its outline with a pencil. Demonstrate as necessary. Have students write the names of their city and state capital in the state.

Follow-up Activities

✪ Ask students about their native countries: "What city are you from?" "Are there states and state capitals?" "What's the national capital?"

✪ Discuss with students the state and local seats of government—state capitol and city hall. Have students identify photographs of the governor and mayor and match them with photographs or names of the places they work. Locate and identify Washington, D.C., and identify a picture of the President.

✪ Discuss the geographic regions of the country—North, South, Midwest, West Coast, and so on. Have students identify and shade in their region on the map.

2 INFORMATION GAP: MAP OF THE U.S.A.

Materials: handouts 2a, 2b

Type of Activity: pair

Language Development: listening, speaking, graphical literacy

INS Questions: 5, 6, 7 (see page 34)

Level: beginning, intermediate

Directions: Using a wall map and/or the map on handout 1, review the geography of the United States. Have students find Canada, Mexico, the largest state, the smallest state, their own state, other states in your region, and so on. Review direction words, size words, and prepositions (above, below, next to, and so on). Then have students work in pairs to complete their individual maps (2a or 2b) by asking their partner questions such as, "Where is Canada?". The partner might then answer, "It's the large country north of the United States." (Write this example on the board, if desired.) Partners should never see each other's maps. They must communicate orally to complete their respective maps.

Follow-up Activities

⭐ Construct a similar information gap map focusing on the states of your region. Use two copies of the map on handout 1 and make deletions before duplicating.

⭐ For more advanced students, prepare an additional set of maps with more than six deletions.

 BINGO: AMERICA

Materials: handouts 3a, 3b, 3c; scissors

Type of Activity: individual or pair

Language Development: listening, speaking, graphical literacy

INS Questions: No questions correspond to this activity.

Level: literacy, beginning, multilevel

Directions: This activity is intended to introduce and practice vocabulary in "America the Beautiful" and "This Land Is Your Land."

Prelistening Map Work. Use the map on handout 3a to prepare your class for Bingo: America. Working as a whole group, locate (and label if students can write) the following:

> mountains (the two major ranges)
> the oceans (Atlantic and Pacific)
> California
> New York
> the Gulf of Mexico
> desert areas (New Mexico and Arizona)
> important islands (Hawaii and Long Island)
> the Great Plains (Kansas, Nebraska, Oklahoma, and so on)

Have beginning-level students label the Great Lakes and the Mississippi River as well.

Follow the directions for Using Bingo.

Using Bingo

Bingo is a versatile activity, well suited to multilevel classes. By using pictures instead of print, bingo provides a positive learning experience for nonliterate, semiliterate, and literate students. *The Uncle Sam Activity Book* uses an innovative twelve-item grid that helps limit content to a manageable amount.

Directions

1. Preplay Activities. To introduce new concepts and vocabulary, distribute one copy of the bingo cutouts to each student (or pair very weak students with stronger ones). If possible, make a transparency of this sheet and project it on the overhead projector. Discuss each picture. Read the cues in order while students listen and point to the items being called. (See Ideas for Cues, next page.) Prompt as necessary. Next, read the cues in random order while students continue to point to items called.

2. Preparing the Bingo Grids. After the Preplay Activities, prepare the bingo grids. This can be done either before class by the teacher or during class by the students as a Total Physical Response (TPR) activity. If you choose to do a TPR activity, say this: "Cut your paper along the lines. Cut twelve squares. Count them (one, two, three, four, five, six, seven, eight, nine, ten, eleven, twelve). Paste (glue, tape) the squares on this paper (the bingo grid, handout 3c). Put one square in each empty square. Put them in a different order from your classmates'. Everyone's paper should be different."

Option for beginning/intermediate levels.

If there is a matchup activity in the unit you are working on, instead of using pictures on the bingo grids, use the terms from the left side of the matchups. Write the terms on the board and have students copy them in random order onto the blank bingo grids. Use the definitions of the terms (right side of matchups) for cues.

Note: To make each round last longer, or to serve as a review, use the bingo cutouts from two or more units when preparing the grids. Doing so increases the pool of cues and makes the game more challenging.

3. Playing the Game. Before beginning the game, decide which of the following four patterns will constitute a win. Draw the target pattern on the board.

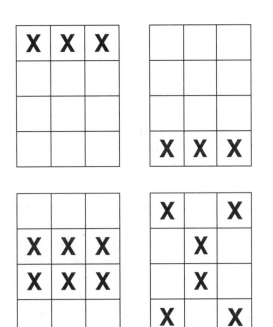

Ideas for Cues

Literacy Level. Give single-term cues: mountains, ocean, forest, valley, California, New York, grain, island, Gulf of Mexico, highway, desert, sky.

Beginning Level. Give definitions or descriptions: It's very hot here (desert), You drive your car on this (highway), One of these is the Pacific (ocean), and so on.

Giving cues. There are two possibilities for giving cues.

A. The *teacher* gives the cues. Ideas for Cues are found in the Teacher's Notes.

B. In a more advanced or multilevel class, *students* give the cues. Cut up a copy of the bingo cutouts and put the items into a box. Have a more advanced student pick an item out of the box and give an appropriate cue. If the other

students don't understand, they must ask for clarification: "Please repeat." "I don't understand." Having students give cues maximizes student talk and fosters spontaneous communication.

Hints for play. So that the grids can be reused, have students cover items with bits of paper. Ask students who get bingo to call out covered items to verify their wins and to get additional speaking practice.

Follow-up Activities

All Levels. Have students compare U.S. geography to that of their native countries (size, topography, weather) in a speaking or writing activity.

Beginning Level. Dictation: "The United States is a big country. It has mountains, plains, and deserts. There are many lakes and rivers. An important river is the Mississippi."

4 WORD CUES: "AMERICA THE BEAUTIFUL"

Materials: handout 4, *The Uncle Sam Activity Tape*, scissors

Type of Activity: whole class

Language Development: listening, sight reading

INS Questions: No questions correspond to this activity.

Level: literacy

Directions: (You may want to do Bingo: America, handouts 3a and 3b, before this activity.) Before listening to the song, write the word cues on the board and go over the meanings. Duplicate enough copies of the handout so that each student or each pair of students will receive one word. (More than one student can have the same word.) Cut the handout on the lines and distribute one word to each student or pair of students.

Call out the words one by one and have the student(s) who has that word either hold the word up high or stand up. Prompt as necessary.

Play the song, pausing after each line. As in the prelistening exercise, when a student hears her or his word, she or he should either hold the word up high or stand up. Redistribute the words and repeat the activity.

Follow-up Activities

⭐ Write the words to the song on the board or pass out copies of the words (see page 40). Have students circle their words.

⭐ Have the class sing the song.

Note: *The Uncle Sam Activity Tape* includes an additional verse. The complete lyrics are found on page 40.

5 MODIFIED CLOZE LISTENING: "AMERICA THE BEAUTIFUL"

Materials: handout 5, *The Uncle Sam Activity Tape*

Type of Activity: individual or pair

Language Development: listening, reading

INS Questions: No questions correspond to this activity.

Level: literacy, beginning, multilevel

Directions: (Before doing this activity, you may want to do Word Cues: "America the Beautiful," handout 4.) Distribute copies of the handout. Go over vocabulary as necessary. Play the song through one time while students listen (have students put down their pencils during this initial playing). Play the song through again, pausing after each line to allow students to circle the correct word. To help nonliterate students,

point out each word as it is sung (have the words written either on the board or on an overhead transparency). Replay the tape as many times as the students request. When students are satisfied with their work, correct the activity together.

Multilevel. For groups with mixed literacy skills, pair weaker students with stronger ones.

Follow-up Activity

⭐ Have the class sing the song.

Note: *The Uncle Sam Activity Tape* includes an additional verse. The complete lyrics are found on page 40.

6 CLOZE LISTENING: "AMERICA THE BEAUTIFUL"

Materials: handout 6, *The Uncle Sam Activity Tape*

Type of Activity: individual

Language Development: listening, speaking

INS Questions: No questions correspond to this activity.

Level: beginning, intermediate, multilevel

Directions: (Before doing this activity, you may want to do Bingo: America handouts 3a and 3b to review vocabulary.) Distribute the handout top to beginning students and the handout bottom to intermediate students (if there are literacy-level students in the class, give the Modified Cloze listening: "America the Beautiful," handout 5). Play the song through one time while students listen (have students put down their pencils during this initial playing). Play the song through again, pausing after each line to allow students time to write the missing words. Replay the tape as many times as the students request. When students are satisfied with their work, correct the activity together.

Follow-up Activity

⭐ Have the class sing the song.

Note: *The Uncle Sam Activity Tape* includes an additional verse. The complete lyrics are found on page 40.

 WORD CUES: "THIS LAND IS YOUR LAND"

Materials: handouts 7a, 7b; *The Uncle Sam Activity Tape*

Type of Activity: whole class

Language Development: listening, sight reading, graphical literacy

INS Questions: No questions correspond to this activity.

Level: literacy, beginning, intermediate, multilevel

Directions: (Before doing this activity, you may want to do Bingo: America, handouts 3a and 3b.)

Prelistening Map Work. Use the map on handout 3a to prepare students for the word cues. Working as a whole group, locate and label the following: California, the redwood forests, New York (Long Island), the Gulf of Mexico, major desert areas (New Mexico and Nevada). Bring in pictures of these places if possible. Find out if any students have been to these places.

Literacy Level. Use only the handout for verse 1 (handout 7a). Follow directions for Word Cues: "America the Beautiful," handout 4.

Beginning/Intermediate Levels. Use the handouts for verse 1 (handout 7a) and verses 2 and 3 (handout 7b). Continue as above.

Multilevel. Give literacy and beginning students words from verse 1 (handout 7a) and intermediate students words from verses 2 and 3 (handout 7b). Continue as above.

Follow-up Activity

⭐ Write the words to the song on the board or pass out copies of the words (page 40). Have the class sing the song.

 CLOZE LISTENING: "THIS LAND IS YOUR LAND"

Materials: handout 8, *The Uncle Sam Activity Tape*

Type of Activity: individual

Language Development: listening, reading, graphical literacy

INS Questions: No questions correspond to this activity.

Level: beginning, intermediate

Directions: Do the Prelistening Map Work on this page to prepare students for this cloze listening.

Then distribute copies of the handout (for beginning-level students, cut off the final two verses). Follow directions for Cloze Listening: "America the Beautiful," page 5. Complete song lyrics are found on page 40.

Follow-up Activities

Beginning/Intermediate Levels.

⭐ Have the class sing the song.

⭐ Have students write a composition describing the places they have visited or would like to visit in the United States.

⭐ Have students prepare a short speech describing a particular place they have visited in the United States.

Intermediate Level. Provide resource materials (books, atlases, travel brochures, magazines, encyclopedias, Internet) on the fifty states. Have students (individually or in small groups) prepare an oral and/or written report on a state of their choice.

9 THE AMERICAN FLAG

Materials: handout 9, an American flag or a colored picture of one

Type of Activity: individual

Language Development: listening

INS Questions: 1, 2, 3, 4, 5, 6, 7, 8, 9, 10, 23, 24 (see pages 34 - 35)

Level: literacy, beginning, intermediate, multilevel

Directions: Using the flag or a colored picture of one, discuss with students the parts of the flag (stars, stripes, field); the meaning of the colors (red for courage, white for truth, blue for justice); the fifty stars (for the fifty states); and the thirteen stripes (for the first thirteen states). Elicit any information they may already have.

Literacy Level. Before duplicating, write the names of the thirteen colonies (one on each of the stripes of the "flag" on the handout bottom) and the numeral 50 in the outline of the U.S.A. in the field. Have students trace over them.

Beginning Level. Write the names of the thirteen colonies on the board. Have students copy them on the stripes and write the numeral 50 inside the outline.

Intermediate Level. Ask students to put the number of states in the outline and dictate the names of the thirteen states to be written on the stripes. (Teacher or students can spell the names if necessary.) Students can also be asked to write in the names from memory. Finished illustrations will look like this:

50	Massachusets
	New Hampshire
	New York
	Connecticut
	Rhode Island
	Pennsylvania
	New Jersey
	Maryland
	Delaware
	Virginia
	North Carolina
	South Carolina
	Georgia

Follow-up Activities

⭐ Have students draw or bring in flags of their native countries. Describe and discuss the flags.

⭐ Bring in, describe, and discuss the flags of your state and city.

10 THE AMERICAN FLAG IN EVERYDAY LIFE

Materials: handout 10, *The Uncle Sam Activity Tape* (optional)

Type of Activity: whole class

Language Development: listening, writing

INS Questions: No questions correspond to this activity.

Level: literacy, beginning, intermediate, multilevel

Directions

All Levels. Using the following script, describe each picture. In the square to the upper left of each picture, have students write the number of the description they hear.

Activity Script (Teacher or Tape):

Number 1 The flag is flying on a mast outside of a school.

Number 2 Flag Day is a holiday in June to honor our flag.

Number 3 When a veteran or soldier dies, a flag is put over the casket.

Number 4 When the nation mourns a death, the flag is flown at half-mast.

Number 5 To show respect, the flag must be folded in a special way.

Number 6 The American flag is often first in a holiday parade.

Answers:

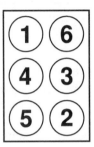

Beginning Level. Have students describe the pictures orally and then write simple sentences about each one on the lines below each picture. Cue words from the script can be put on the board for assistance.

Intermediate Level. Have students describe the pictures orally and then write a paragraph on the flag in American life. Alternatively, have students write from dictation the sentences from the activity script on the lines below each picture.

Follow-up Activities

⭐ Discuss other examples of the flag in everyday life (where they see it flown; use at the Olympics, sports events, public meetings, and so on).

⭐ Have students bring in pictures of the American flag as they find them on everyday items (newspapers, campaign literature, and so on).

⭐ Discuss the symbolic meaning of the flag and the controversy that may surround it (for example, flag burning).

11 CLOZE: THE PLEDGE OF ALLEGIANCE

Materials: handout 11, *The Uncle Sam Activity Tape* (optional)

Type of Activity: individual

Language Development: listening, reading

INS Questions: 41 (see page 35)

Level: beginning, intermediate, multilevel

Directions: Explain the purpose and meaning of the pledge through key vocabulary (*pledge, allegiance, republic, indivisible, liberty, justice*). Discuss what is meant by a republican government (a government in which the people rule through freely elected representatives and an elected chief executive who are responsible to the people).

Distribute handout 11. With papers face down, have students listen to the pledge (teacher or tape). Have them turn over their papers and write in the correct prepositions. Repeat the pledge as necessary.

Activity Script (Teacher or Tape): I pledge allegiance to the flag of the United States of America and to the Republic for which it stands, one Nation, under God, indivisible, with liberty and justice for all.

Follow-up Activities

⭐ Discuss loyalty to the flag in other countries.

⭐ Dictate the pledge of allegiance as a writing activity.

⭐ Discuss the symbolic meaning of the flag and the controversy that may surround it (for example, flag burning).

⭐ Construct other cloze activities with the pledge by deleting key vocabulary.

UNIT 2
Columbus and the New World

12 PICTURE SEQUENCING ACTIVITY: CHRISTOPHER COLUMBUS

Materials: handouts 12a, 12b; *The Uncle Sam Activity Tape* (optional)

Type of Activity: individual

Language Development: listening, writing

INS Questions: No questions correspond to this activity.

Level: literacy, beginning, multilevel

Directions: Using the world map on handout 12a, have students locate Italy, Spain, Asia, and North America. Briefly tell students the story of Columbus or elicit this information from them. On the world map, trace the path of Columbus' first voyage (from Spain to San Salvador in the West Indies). Then follow the script below and have students number the pictures on handout 12b in the squares to the upper left as they listen.

Activity Script (Teacher or Tape):

Number 1 Christopher Columbus was a sailor and explorer from Italy. He studied the winds and ocean.

Number 2 He wanted to sail west to find a new way to Asia.

Number 3 He asked the king and queen of Spain for help.

Number 4 They gave him three ships— the *Niña*, the *Pinta*, and the *Santa Maria.*

Number 5 He discovered the new land of America in 1492.

Number 6 Because he thought he had reached India, he called the native people Indians.

Answers:

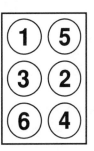

Follow-up Activities

Literacy Level. Cut out the pictures and have students place them in the correct order as they listen. Then have them practice retelling the story to a partner, who puts the pictures in the correct order.

Beginning Level. Have students write sentences telling the story on the lines below each picture. Provide a word bank on the board with key vocabulary if necessary.

Intermediate Level. After the prelistening map work, have students tell you the story using the pictures as cues. Then have them write a paragraph about Columbus and his discovery. Alternatively, have students write from dictation the sentences from the activity script on the lines below each picture.

13 STRIP STORY: CHRISTOPHER COLUMBUS AND THE NEW WORLD

Materials: handout 13, scissors

Type of Activity: whole class or individual

Language Development: listening, speaking, reading, sequencing

INS Questions: No questions correspond to this activity.

Level: beginning, intermediate

Directions: Using Strip Stories

Strip stories strengthen reading comprehension and sequencing skills as students work together as a group or individually.

Type of Activity: whole class

1. Preparing for the Activity

Duplicate enough copies of the handout so that each student will receive one sentence (if necessary, divide the class into two groups or have students work in pairs). Introduce or review vocabulary and discuss the historical content as necessary. Use pictures from related handouts to help convey content.

2. Conducting the Activity

Beginning Level. Distribute copies of the handout (story intact) to students before giving out the strips. Have students read the story silently; then ask comprehension questions. Read the story to the class, having students repeat each sentence to practice pronunciation. Collect the handouts and distribute the strips. Have students read their strips aloud one by one and then work as a group to put the story in order.

Intermediate Level. Do not distribute the story before distributing the strips. Instead, read the story (once or twice) to the group and then have students assemble the story as above.

Type of Activity: individual (intermediate level)

Directions: Duplicate one handout for each student. After an appropriate review, give each student an envelope containing story strips and have students work independently to put their strips in order.

Note for Multilevel Classes: Keep several envelopes of strip stories on hand for advanced students to do individually when they finish an activity before the rest of the class. Provide a copy of the handout for self-correction.

Follow-up Activities

Beginning/Intermediate Levels. Prepare a cloze exercise by deleting key vocabulary from the handout before duplicating it. Have students read the story and fill in the missing words.

Intermediate Level. Dictate selected sentences of the strip story to the class for writing practice.

14 BINGO: EARLY SETTLERS

Materials: handout 14, scissors

Type of Activity: individual or pair

Language Development: listening, speaking

INS Questions: 11, 12, 13, 14 (see page 34)

Level: literacy, beginning, multilevel

Directions: See Using Bingo, pages 3–4

Ideas for Cues. The matchups on Matchup: Early Settlers, handout 15, correspond to the pictures on Bingo: Early Settlers. Use either the terms on the left side of the matchups or the definitions on the right for bingo cues.

Follow-up Activity

⭐ Language Experience Story. Have students retell the story of the Pilgrims in their own words as you help them form sentences and write them on the board. Practice reading the story, chorally and individually. Have students copy the story and use it for additional reading practice.

15 MATCHUPS: EARLY SETTLERS

Materials: handout 15

Type of Activity: whole class

Language Activity: listening, speaking, reading

INS Questions: 11, 12, 13, 14 (see page 34)

Level: literacy, beginning, intermediate, multilevel

Directions: Using Matchups

Matchups get students on their feet in a communicative mixer activity. Matchups also result in assignment of random pairs for follow-up activities.

Literacy Level. Make two copies of the bingo cutouts on handout 14 (more if the class has over 24 students). Put the pictures in a box, and have each student pick one at random. Cut out only enough matching pairs of pictures as there are pairs of students in the class. Have students circulate and find their partners with the same picture only by describing their pictures to one another. Students should not see one another's pictures except to verify the match.

Beginning/Intermediate Levels. Duplicate the sentence matchups and cut out the number of matchups needed for two students per sentence. (If there is an odd number of students, the teacher should play.) Cut each sentence in half as indicated. Put all the slips into a box and let each student pick one slip at random. Have students read their strips to one another (without looking at each other's strips) to find the correct match.

Multilevel. Use both the sentences from the matchups and the pictures from the bingo cutouts. Divide these into two boxes: pictures for literacy students and words for beginning and intermediate students. Have students circulate and form three-way matchups.

For all levels, check the activity together. Have students read their sentences (for example, The *Mayflower* was the Pilgrims' ship.) and/or describe their pictures (for example, This is the *Mayflower.*).

Follow-up Activities

⭐ **Review Questions.** Use the terms on the left side of the matchup handout to ask the class questions (for example, *Mayflower*, "What was the *Mayflower*?").

⭐ **What's the Question?** Cut out only the strips of terms on the left side of the matchup handout. In small groups, students can each pick a term at random and give the *question* for the answer (for example, *Mayflower*, "What was the Pilgrims' ship?"). The exact content of the matchups need not be reflected in students' questions as long as the questions and answers correctly review civics content.

⭐ **Thumbs Up—Thumbs Down.** Use the complete sentences of the matchups. Duplicate one copy to use as your script. Change some of the sentences to reflect incorrect content. In a listening comprehension review exercise for the whole class, instruct students to show *thumbs up* after you read a true statement and *thumbs down* after you read a false one. (Example: "The *Santa Maria* was the Pilgrims' ship." Students show thumbs down. "The *Mayflower* was the Pilgrims' ship." Students show thumbs up.)

⭐ **Dictation.** Dictate some of the matchup sentences for listening and writing practice.

⭐ **Scrambled Sentences.** Using complete sentences from the matchups, design scrambled sentences that students must put in correct word order (for example, ship *Mayflower* the was The Pilgrims'→ The *Mayflower* was the Pilgrims' ship).

⭐ **Matchup Variation.** Use the matchups for a memory game for pairs.

Literacy Level. Duplicate two copies of the bingo cutouts (from a unit of your choice) for each pair of students. Pictures are cut out and turned face down. One of the students turns over any two pictures. If the pictures do not match, they are returned to their original position. If the student picks up a match, he or she must identify the pictures. Then the student can keep them and take another turn. The second player repeats the process. The student who picks up the most pairs of pictures wins.

Beginning Level. Use the pictures from the bingo cutouts and the terms from the left side of the sentence matchups. Mount all the pictures and terms on index cards. Have students match the pictures to the correct terms. Play as above.

Beginning/Intermediate Levels. Use only the sentence matchups. Mount the terms from the left side and the definitions from the right side on index cards if desired. Play as above.

Multilevel. Prepare different envelopes of matchups for each level, as above. Distribute envelopes to pairs according to level.

16 SKIT: THE PILGRIMS IN AMERICA

Materials: handouts 16a, 16b; table, three chairs, cross, corn kernels, rolled paper (for document), feather (for quill pen)

Type of Activity: whole class

Language Development: listening, speaking, reading

INS Questions: 11, 12, 13, 14 (see page 34)

Level: intermediate, multilevel

Directions: Using Skits

Skits provide content reinforcement through role-playing. Gestures and props help convey meaning as students bring history to life in the classroom.

Elicit from the class what they already know about the historical period of the skit. Preview unfamiliar vocabulary and teach in context. Summarize the story. Read the skit to the class, modeling pronunciation and expression. Read it again, having students repeat chorally. Assign tasks according to students' abilities and interests: roles, stage setup, props, and so on. Have actors rehearse; memorizing lines is not necessary. While actors are rehearsing, the rest of the class can be rereading the skit. The play can be performed either for your class or for another ESL class. It can be staged again with different students.

Note: Advanced students may be able to improvise during the skit or as a follow-up activity.

Follow-up Activities

⭐ Class Discussion.

- Discuss how the class feels about religious freedom as a reason for emigration.

- Discuss the Mayflower Compact as an early forerunner of the Constitution.

- Discuss the relationship between the Pilgrims and the Native Americans.

⭐ In-Character Composition. Have students write a composition or journal entry (individually or in small groups) as Pilgrims describing their thoughts and feelings about leaving England, the Mayflower Compact, or the first Thanksgiving. (This would be a first-person present-tense composition.)

⭐ News Report. Have students cover the events of the skit by giving an oral newscast in the present continuous tense.

⭐ Newspaper Article. Have students (individually or in small groups) write an article about the events in the skit. They will use the five *wh-'s*: *who, what, where, when,* and *why.*

17 STRIP STORY: THE FIRST THANKSGIVING

Materials: handout 17, scissors

Type of Activity: whole class or individual

Language Development: listening, speaking, reading, sequencing

INS Questions: 11, 12, 13, 14 (see page 34)

Level: beginning, intermediate

Directions: See Using Strip Stories, page 10.

UNIT 4
Independence from England

18 INFORMATION GAP: MAP OF THE THIRTEEN COLONIES

Materials: handouts 18a, 18b, 18c

Type of Activity: pair

Language Development: listening, speaking, graphical literacy

INS Questions: 23, 24 (see page 35)

Level: beginning, intermediate

Directions: Using the map on handout 18a, discuss (elicit from the students if possible) the development of the early English colonies. (By 1733 there were thirteen distinct colonies in the New World.) Practice pronouncing the names of the thirteen colonies. Review direction words, (*north, south, east, west*), size words, and prepositions (*above, below, next to*, and so on). Then have students work in pairs to complete their maps (18b or 18c) by asking their partner questions such as, "Where's Georgia?". The partner might respond, "It's the colony south of South Carolina." (Write this example on the board, if desired.) Partners should never see each other's maps. They must communicate orally to complete their respective maps.

19 SKIT: LET FREEDOM RING!

Materials: handouts 19a, 19b, 19c; table, five chairs, paper, feather (for quill pen), rope with noose, bell

Type of Activity: whole class

Language Development: listening, speaking, reading

INS Questions: 16, 17, 18, 19, 20, 21, 22 (see page 34 - 35)

Level: intermediate, multilevel

Directions: See Using Skits, pages 12–13. Discuss the events leading up to the Declaration of Independence (high taxes, Boston Tea Party, loss of trade, start of Revolutionary War, and so on).

Follow-up Activities

✪ Class Discussion. Discuss other nations that were once colonies that fought for independence. Noting the absence of women as political leaders during the colonial period, discuss how this has changed since 1776.

✪ In-Character Composition. Have students (individually or in small groups) write a composition or journal entry as one of the characters in the skit. Have them write a persuasive composition giving reasons for remaining a part of or for separating from England.

✪ News Report. Have students cover the events of the Second Continental Congress by giving an *oral* newscast in the present continuous tense.

✪ Newspaper Article. Have students (individually or in small groups) write an article about the writing of the Declaration of Independence. Have them use the five *wh-'s*: *who, what, where, when*, and *why*.

✪ Speech. Have students play the role of King George giving a speech after he gets the Declaration of Independence. Students should prepare the speech in advance.

✪ Heroes from Other Countries. Have students research and report on Revolutionary War heroes from other countries who helped the American cause; for example, Pulaski from Poland, von Steuben from Germany, and Lafayette from France.

✪ Listening Activities: "My Country 'Tis of Thee" below.

20 SCRAMBLED SONG: "MY COUNTRY 'TIS OF THEE"

Materials: handout 20, *The Uncle Sam Activity Tape*, scissors

Type of Activity: individual or pair

Language Development: listening, reading, predicting

INS Questions: No questions correspond to this activity.

Level: beginning, intermediate

Directions: Duplicate one copy of handout 20 for each student or pair of students. Cut (or have students cut) along the dotted lines and put the strips into an envelope. Before distributing the envelopes, introduce key vocabulary from the song. Give each student or pair of students an envelope with the strips mixed up inside. Give students a few minutes to read through the strips. Play the song through, pausing after each line while students put the strips in order. Replay the song as many times as the students request. Correct the assembling of the strips together.

Follow-up Activity

✪ Have the class sing the song.

Note: *The Uncle Sam Activity Tape* includes an additional verse. The complete lyrics are found on page 40.

21 CARET LISTENING: "MY COUNTRY 'TIS OF THEE"

Materials: handout 21, *The Uncle Sam Activity Tape*

Type of Activity: individual

Language Development: listening, reading

INS Questions: No questions correspond to this activity.

Level: beginning, intermediate

Directions: Before distributing handout 21, introduce key vocabulary from the song. Then have students listen to the song and put a caret (∧) wherever a word is missing. (The first line is done for them.) Stop the tape after each line to help students complete the task. More advanced students can write the missing words above the carets. Replay the tape as many times as the students request. When they are satisfied with their work, ask them how many carets there are (there should be six). If there is a discrepancy, replay the tape. Correct the activity together.

Answers:

My country 'tis ∧ thee
Sweet land ∧ liberty
Of thee ∧ sing.
Land where ∧ fathers died,
Land ∧ the Pilgrims' pride,
∧ every mountain side
Let freedom ring.
Total: six

Follow-up Activity

⭐ Have the class sing the song.

Note: *The Uncle Sam Activity Tape* includes an additional verse. The complete lyrics are found on page 40.

22 STRIP STORY: FRANCIS SCOTT KEY AND "THE STAR-SPANGLED BANNER"

Materials: handout 22, scissors

Type of Activity: whole class or individual

Language Development: listening, speaking, reading, sequencing

INS Questions: 27, 28 (see page 35)

Level: beginning, intermediate

Directions: See Using Strip Stories, page 10.

Follow-up Activities

⭐ See suggested follow-up activities for Listening Activity: "The Star-Spangled Banner," handout 23.

23 LISTENING ACTIVITY: "THE STAR-SPANGLED BANNER"

Materials: handout 23, *The Uncle Sam Activity Tape*

Type of Activity: individual

Language Development: listening, reading

INS Questions: 27, 28 (see page 35)

Level: beginning, intermediate

Directions: (Before doing this activity you may want to do the Strip Story: Francis Scott Key and "The Star-Spangled Banner" on handout 22.) Duplicate one handout for each student. Before distributing the handouts, introduce key vocabulary from the song. Then have students listen to the song and put a caret (∧) wherever a word is missing. (The first line is done for them.) Stop the tape for a few seconds after each line to help students complete the task. More advanced students can write the missing words above the carets. Replay the tape as many times as the students request. When they are satisfied with their work, ask them how many carets they marked (there should be twenty-two). If there is a discrepancy, replay the tape. Distribute copies of the song (page 41) and clarify any problems.

Answers:

Oh say can ∧ see, (1)
by ∧ dawn's early light, (1)
What so proudly ∧ hailed (1)
at ∧ twilight's ∧ gleaming. (2)
Whose broad stripes ∧ bright ∧ (2)
through ∧ perilous fight, (1)
O'er the ramparts ∧ watched (1)
were ∧ gallantly streaming; (1)
And the rockets' ∧ glare, (1)
∧ bombs bursting ∧ air, (2)
Gave proof ∧ the night (1)
that ∧ flag was ∧ there. (2)
Oh ∧ does ∧ star-spangled (2)
banner yet wave (0)
O'er ∧ land of ∧ free (2)
and ∧ home ∧ the brave? (2)
Total: twenty-two.

Follow-up Activities

⭐ Have students from the same country bring in a recording of or sing their country's national anthem for the class. Do they know the story behind their national anthem? When and where is it sung or played? When and where do Americans sing the national anthem?

⭐ Have the class sing "The Star-Spangled Banner."

Note: *The Uncle Sam Activity Tape* includes an additional verse. The complete lyrics are found on page 41.

UNIT 5
The Constitution and Civil Rights

24 SKIT: WE THE PEOPLE

Materials: handouts 24a, 24b, 24c; table, five chairs, rolled paper, feather (for quill pen)

Type of Activity: whole class

Language Development: listening, speaking

INS Questions: 23, 24, 35, 36, 37, 38, 39, 40, 42, 43, 88 (see pages 35 and 37)

Level: intermediate, multilevel

Directions: Ask students if their native countries have constitutions. Are they similar to the United States Constitution? What is the "law of the land" in their countries?

See Using Skits, pages 12–13.

Follow-up Activities

 Class Discussion.

- Discuss the conditions that led to the writing of the Constitution.

- Discuss how the Constitution differed from the Articles of Confederation.

- Discuss other issues debated at the Constitutional Convention—slavery, civil rights, and so on.

✪ In-Character Composition. Have students (individually or in small groups) write a composition or journal entry as a leader at the Constitutional Convention. They can write persuasive compositions giving reasons for their stand on a certain issue.

✪ News Report. Have students role-play an interview between a reporter and one of the convention leaders.

✪ Newspaper Article. Have students (individually or in small groups) write an article about the Constitutional Convention. Have them use the five *wh-'s: who, what, where, when,* and *why.*

25 BINGO: RIGHTS AND DUTIES OF CITIZENS

Materials: handout 25, scissors

Type of Activity: individual or pair

Language Development: listening, speaking

INS Questions: 45, 46, 47, 48, 49, 50, 51, 52, 53 (see pages 35–36)

Level: literacy, beginning, multilevel

Directions: See Using Bingo, pages 3–4.

Ideas for Cues. The matchups on Matchups: Rights and Duties of Citizens, handout 26, correspond to the pictures on Bingo: Rights and Duties of Citizens. Use either the terms on the left side of the matchups or the definitions on the right for bingo cues.

26 MATCHUPS: RIGHTS AND DUTIES OF CITIZENS

Materials: handout 26

Type of Activity: whole class

Language Development: listening, speaking, reading

INS Questions: 45, 46, 47, 48, 49, 50, 51, 52, 53 (see pages 35–36)

Level: literacy, beginning, intermediate, multilevel

Directions: See Using Matchups, pages 11–12.

Follow-up Activities

⭐ Discuss the Bill of Rights and use the bingo cutouts on handout 25 to help convey content.

⭐ Review the rights, benefits, and duties of citizenship in the United States

27 APPLICATION ACTIVITY: THE BILL OF RIGHTS

Materials: handouts 27a, 27b

Type of Activity: small group or individual

Language Development: listening, speaking, reading

INS Questions: 45, 46, 47, 48, 49, 50 (see pages 35–36)

Level: literacy, beginning, intermediate

Directions: (You may want to do Bingo: Rights and Duties of Citizens and Matchups: Rights and Duties of Citizens, handouts 25 and 26, before doing this activity.) Review the concept of amendments and the Constitution as a "living document." Elicit from students what basic rights are guaranteed by the Constitution. Distribute handout 27a and discuss Amendments 1–10. Then distribute handout 27b and have students work in groups of four to six (or individually) to complete the application activity.

Answers:

1. First Amendment
2. Eighth
3. Second
4. First
5. First
6. Fourth
7. Sixth
8. First

Follow-up Activities

⭐ Discuss which of these situations should *not* happen (2, José Lopez's being fined $300 for an illegal left turn, and 6, the police searching Tony Martin's apartment without permission.) Why?

⭐ Have each group think of two more situations that should *not* happen because of rights protected by the Bill of Rights.

28 CHART READING: CIVIL RIGHTS LEADERS

Materials: handouts 28a, 28b

Type of Activity: small group or individual

Language Development: graphical literacy, scanning

INS Questions: 29, 30, 31, 33 (see page 35)

Level: beginning, intermediate

Directions: Discuss the concept of civil rights and give examples. Guide students in scanning the chart for specific information. Then have students work together in groups of four to six (or individually) to answer the questions.

Answers:

1. Lincoln
2. King
3. Kennedy
4. King
5. Lincoln, Kennedy, and King
6. Lincoln

7. improved civil rights, housing, and education

8. for using nonviolence to achieve equality

9. Lincoln, Kennedy, and King

10. almost three years

11. fifty-six years old

12. forty-six years old

13. thirty-nine years old

14. Lincoln

Follow-up Activities

Beginning/Intermediate Levels

⭐ Discussion.

- How have civil rights improved in the United States since the time of Lincoln?

- What civil rights issues exist in students' native countries?

- Who are/were some civil rights leaders in their countries?

Intermediate Level

Provide reference materials and have students choose one of the three leaders as the subject of an oral or written report.

29 SCRAMBLED SONG: ABRAHAM, MARTIN, AND JOHN

Materials: handout 29, *The Uncle Sam Activity Tape*, scissors

Type of Activity: individual or pair

Language Development: listening, reading, predicting

INS Questions: 29, 30, 31, 33 (see page 35)

Level: beginning, intermediate

Directions: (Before doing this activity, you may want to do Chart Reading: Civil Rights Leaders, handouts 28a and 28b.)

Duplicate one copy of handout 29 for each student or pair of students. Cut (or have students cut) along the dotted lines and put the strips into an envelope.

Give each student or pair of students an envelope with the strips mixed up inside. Give the students several minutes to sort the strips by symbols, (circles, triangles, squares, stars, and diamonds), read through the strips, begin predicting what they are going to hear, and find the title. Have students put the title at the top. Cue students before playing each verse by saying, "Now listen for the circles" (triangles, squares, and so on). Play the song through, pausing after each line while students put the strips in order. Replay the song as many times as the students request. Distribute copies of the words (page 41) and have students check their work. Clarify any problems.

Intermediate Level. To make the activity more challenging, cut off the symbols (stanza markers) on each line before listening to the song.

Follow-up Activities

⭐ Have the class sing the song.

⭐ See Follow-up Activities for Chart Reading: Civil Rights Leaders, next page.

30 CHART READING: MORE CIVIL RIGHTS LEADERS

Materials: handouts 30a, 30b

Type of Activity: small group or individual

Language Development: graphical literacy, scanning

INS Questions: 42, 43, 44, 89, 90, 91 (see pages 35 and 38)

Level: beginning, intermediate

Directions: Discuss the concept of civil rights and give examples. Guide students in scanning the chart for specific information. Then have students work together in groups of four to six (or individually) to answer the questions.

Answers:

1. a person who worked to give women the right to vote
2. a person who worked to end slavery
3. Tubman
4. Anthony
5. Anthony, for trying to vote; Parks, for refusing to give up her seat to a white passenger
6. Parks
7. 381 days
8. Tubman
9. Tubman
10. 1920
11. gave women the right to vote
12. Anthony, Tubman, and Parks

Follow-up Activities

Beginning/Intermediate Levels

⭐ Discussion

- Discuss the role women play in U.S. politics today. Does your state have any female senators? representatives? Discuss Sandra Day O'Connor (first woman Supreme Court justice) and Geraldine Ferraro (first woman to run for vice president) as examples of women's progress in U.S. politics.

- Discuss the role of women in politics in students' native countries. Do men and women have equal rights?

- Who are/were some female civil rights leaders in their countries?

Intermediate Level

- Discuss the concept of the Underground Railroad. Explain that Harriet Tubman was one of its most active "conductors,"

leading slaves north by night, following the "drinking gourd" (the north star). If possible, bring in a copy of the spiritual "Follow the Drinking Gourd" to class and have students listen to and then sing the song.

- Provide reference materials and have students choose one of these three American women as the subject of an oral or written report.

31 CLOZE LISTENING: "AMERICAN WOMEN: A TRIBUTE TO SUSAN B. ANTHONY, HARRIET TUBMAN, AND ROSA PARKS"

Materials: handout 31, *The Uncle Sam Activity Tape*

Type of Activity: individual

Language Development: listening, reading

INS Questions: No questions correspond to this activity.

Level: beginning, intermediate

Directions: (Before doing this activity, you may want to do Chart Reading: More Civil Rights Leaders, handouts 30a and 30b.)

Duplicate one copy of handout 31 for each student. Distribute copies of the handout. Play the song through one time while students listen (have students put down their pencils during this initial playing). Play the song through again as students write the missing words. (Note: On the tape, each sentence is sung twice while on handout 31 each sentence appears only once.) Replay the tape as many times as the students request. When students are satisfied with their work, correct the activity together.

Follow-up Activity

⭐ Have the class sing the song (complete lyrics are found on page 41).

UNIT 6
Government

32 CHART: YOUR FEDERAL LEADERS

Materials: handout 32

Type of Activity: individual

Language Development: reading, writing

INS Questions: 39, 40, 55, 72, 73, 83, 84 (see pages 35–37)

Level: beginning, intermediate, multilevel

Directions: Review the three branches of government and current federal office holders. Have students identify photographs of these officials if possible.

Beginning Level. Provide a word bank of names on the board to assist students in completing the chart.

Intermediate Level. Have students complete the chart without assistance.

Follow-up Activity

⭐ Discuss the order of Presidential succession—the Vice President becomes President if the President dies; the Speaker of the House becomes President if both the President and the Vice President should die.

33 CHART READING: THE THREE BRANCHES OF GOVERNMENT

Materials: handout 33

Type of Activity: small group or individual

Language Development: graphical literacy, scanning

INS Questions: 40, 54, 55, 62, 65, 67, 68, 71, 82, 92 (see pages 35–38)

Level: intermediate

Directions: Review the three branches of government and guide students in scanning the chart for specific information. Then have students work together in groups of four to six (or individually) to answer the questions.

Answers:

1. legislative, executive, and judicial
2. President, Vice President, and cabinet and cabinet departments
3. 9 Supreme Court justices
4. for life
5. no limit to terms
6. at least 7 years
7. no limit to terms
8. Congress
9. at least 35 years old
10. 14 years

Follow-up Activities

⭐ Have students write complete sentences about the three branches of government based on the information in the chart.

⭐ Construct hypothetical candidates based on the information in the chart (for example, John Smith is a thirty-year-old lawyer born in Utah. He has lived there all his life.). Have students decide what offices these candidates can run for.

⭐ Devise an information gap activity

based on this chart. Partners' charts will have different deletions. Partners practice using *wh-* questions to find out the information missing from their charts.

 LISTENING ACTIVITY: GOVERNMENT NUMBERS

Materials: handout 34 (fill in number of representatives from your state in last column of item 6 before duplicating), *The Uncle Sam Activity Tape* (optional)

Type of Activity: individual

Language Development: listening

INS Questions: 62, 63, 64, 67, 68, 78, 79, 93 (see pages 36–38)

Level: beginning, intermediate

Directions: Distribute the handout. Follow either the literacy level or the beginning/intermediate script below, based on your students' abilities.

Activity Script (Teacher or Tape)

Literacy Level. Read the sentences or play the tape. Have students listen and circle the number they hear.

1. There are _2_ senators from each state.
2. There are _100_ senators in Congress.
3. Senators are elected for _6_ years.
4. There are _435_ representatives in Congress.
5. Representatives are elected for _2_ years.
6. There are ___ representatives in Congress from _____ (your state).
7. There are _9_ Supreme Court justices.
8. The President is elected for _4_ years.
9. The President can serve no more than _2_ terms.
10. The cabinet has _13_ members.

Beginning/Intermediate Levels. Read each question or play the tape. Have students listen and circle the correct answer.

1. How many senators are from each state? (2)
2. How many senators are there in Congress? (100)
3. For how long do we elect each senator? (6 years)
4. How many representatives are there in Congress? (435)
5. For how long do we elect the representatives? (2 years)
6. How many representatives are from _____ (your state)? (varies)
7. How many Supreme Court justices are there? (9)
8. For how long do we elect the President? (4 years)
9. How many terms can a President serve? (2)
10. How many members are in the President's cabinet? (13)

Note: The above questions are worded as they appear on the "INS Questions on History and Government of the U.S." (see Appendix A). However, since the wording of the questions may vary from interview to interview, it is advisable to ask the questions in various ways (for example, item 3 could be stated, "How many years does a senator serve?").

35 LISTENING ACTIVITY: THE THREE BRANCHES OF GOVERNMENT

Materials: handout 35, *The Uncle Sam Activity Tape* (optional)

Type of Activity: individual

Language Development: listening, graphical literacy

INS Questions: 40, 54, 55, 58, 59, 60, 71, 85, 86, 87, 89, 91, 93 (see pages 35–38)

Level: literacy, beginning, intermediate, multilevel

Directions: (Before doing this activity, you may want to do Chart Reading: The Three Branches of Government, handout 33.) With your students, discuss the branches of government, including the powers of each. Then read the questions below. Have students listen and put an X in the appropriate column on the handout.

Activity Script (Teacher or Tape)

1. Which branch makes the laws? (legislative)

2. Which branch hears and judges court cases? (judicial)

3. Who chooses the cabinet members? (executive branch: President)

4. Which branch can remove the President? (legislative)

5. Which branch can remove a Supreme Court justice? (legislative)

6. Which branch can enforce (make people obey) the law? (executive)

7. Who can decide if a law is unconstitutional? (judicial branch)

8. Who can declare war? (legislative branch)

9. Which branch can interpret the law (can decide what a law means)? (judicial)

10. Who commands the U.S. military? (executive branch: President)

11. Who signs bills into laws? (executive branch: President)

12. Who selects the Supreme Court justices? (executive branch: President)

Follow-up Activities

Intermediate Level

⭐ Have students write a short paragraph for each branch of government describing its powers.

⭐ Discuss the system of checks and balances inherent in the structure of the U.S. government.

36 MATCHUPS: THE THREE BRANCHES OF GOVERNMENT

Materials: handout 36 (Write the names of the current president and vice president in the first two left-hand boxes before duplicating.)

Type of Activity: whole class

Language Development: listening, speaking, reading

INS Questions: 54, 59, 62, 64, 67, 68, 70, 71, 72, 73, 87, 89, 92, 94
(see pages 36–38)

Level: beginning, intermediate

Directions: See Using Matchups, pages 11–12. (No bingo cutout pictures correlate to this unit.)

37 BINGO: GOVERNMENT SITES AND SYMBOLS

Materials: handout 37

Type of Activity: individual or pair

Language Development: listening, speaking

INS Questions: 1, 56, 67, 74, 75, 76, 89, 90
(see pages 34 and 36–37)

Level: beginning, multilevel

Directions: See Using Bingo, pages 3–4.

Ideas for Cues. The matchups on Matchups: Government Sites and Symbols, handout 38, correspond to the pictures on Bingo:

Government Sites and Symbols. Use either the terms on the left side of the matchups or the definitions on the right for bingo cues.

38 MATCHUPS: GOVERNMENT SITES AND SYMBOLS

Materials: handout 38

Type of Activity: whole class

Language Development: listening, speaking, reading

INS Questions: 1, 56, 67, 74, 75, 76, 89, 90 (see pages 34 and 36–38)

Level: beginning, intermediate, multilevel

Directions: See Using Matchups, pages 11–12.

Follow-up Activities

✪ Use money as an instant history lesson. Have students find these sites and symbols on U.S. coins and bills.

- Great Seal, back of dollar bill and Kennedy half-dollar
- White House, back of twenty-dollar bill
- Capitol, back of fifty-dollar bill
- Independence Hall, back of hundred-dollar bill

✪ Have partners find out additional information about their site or symbol and present it to the class.

39 LISTENING TO THE NEWS

Materials: handout 39, *The Uncle Sam Activity Tape* (optional)

Type of Activity: individual

Language Development: listening, graphical literacy

INS Questions: 56, 57, 70, 72, 73, 74, 75, 76, 95, 98 (see pages 36–38)

Level: beginning, intermediate, multilevel

Directions: Using handout 39, review the vocabulary (from either the top half or the whole page, depending on level). Follow the appropriate Activity Script (Teacher or Tape) as students listen and have them put an X in front of the words each time they hear them. Repeat as many times as the students request. Correct the activity together.

Activity Script (Teacher or Tape) (Beginning Level)

Washington, D.C. Today at the White House, the President announced his plan to lower taxes. Governors and mayors from state and local governments heard the speech. Tomorrow, Congress will talk about the President's plan at the Capitol here in Washington. Join us tomorrow for this story.

Activity Script (Teacher or Tape) (Intermediate Level) Follow above script and continue:

Washington, D.C. Today Congress gave its reaction to the President's plan to lower taxes. Several representatives said that the President's plan will raise the national debt. Republicans said that the President's proposal does not lower taxes enough. Democrats expressed concern that the tax plan is not as important as the growing pollution problem. In other news, the Vice President will attend a meeting tomorrow with leaders from the Middle East to discuss the price of oil. Join us tomorrow for this story.

Answers:

Beginning Level

_XX_ President

_X_ Governor

_X_ Mayor

_X_ Congress

_XX_ Washington, D.C.

_X_ the White House

_X_ the Capitol

_X_ taxes

Intermediate Level

XXXXX President   _X_ the White House

_X_ Vice President   _X_ the Capitol

_X_ Governor   _X_ the Middle East

_XX_ Congress   _XXXX_ taxes

_X_ Representatives   _X_ meeting

_X_ Republicans   _X_ pollution

_X_ Democrats   _X_ debt

XXX Washington, D.C.

Other Topics

_X_ oil

Follow-up Activities

⭐ For homework, have students listen to the news on radio or TV and fill out handout 39 (you may want to fill in the name of the current President, Vice President, mayor, governor, and state capital on the blank lines before duplicating). Intermediate students can use the blanks on the bottom of the page to record other people, places, and topics they hear. Students then report to the class which words they heard.

⭐ Develop additional "broadcast" scripts based on the current local, national, and international news. Have students use handout 39 or develop your own.

⭐ Tape radio newscasts for in-class guided listening practice.

40 GOVERNMENT IN THE NEWSPAPER

Materials: handouts 40a, 40b, 40c

Type of Activity: small group

Language Development: listening, speaking, reading, writing

INS Questions: 56, 57, 67, 72, 73, 75, 76, 77, 80, 81, 92, 94 (see pages 36–38)

Levels: beginning, intermediate

Directions: Duplicate one set of handouts for each small group of four to six students. Distribute the photos and ask groups to identify the branch of government and/or people pictured. Then distribute the headlines and captions and have students work together to match pictures with the correct captions and headlines. Have students cut the strips and place them on the correct picture.

Intermediate Level. Have students either (1) match the headlines and pictures but write their own captions or (2) match the captions and pictures but write their own headlines.

Follow-up Activities

Intermediate Level

⭐ Have students write corresponding newspaper articles with the five wh-'s: who, what, when, where, and why.

⭐ Have students bring in additional photos from newspapers and magazines for similar activities, or bring them in yourself.

41 CHART: STATE AND LOCAL LEADERS

Materials: handouts 1, 41

Type of Activity: individual

Language Development: sight reading, graphical literacy, writing

INS Questions: 95, 96, 97, 98, 99 (see page 38)

Level: literacy, beginning, intermediate

Directions: Have students locate their state and write in their state capital on the map on handout 1. On a state map, have students locate their capital, their county, and their city. Ask students to name and identify photos of state and local leaders.

Literacy Level. Before duplicating handout 41, write in the information on the top half of the page. Have students trace over the words. To help students relate this content to life skills, have them complete the personal information form on the bottom of the handout.

Beginning Level. Provide a word bank on the board to help students complete the page.

Intermediate Level. Have students complete the page without assistance.

Follow-up Activity

⭐ Provide resource materials and have students find out who their state senators and representatives are. (The state handbook is helpful for this information.)

Unit 7
The Civil War

42 BINGO: THE CIVIL WAR

Materials: handouts 1, 42; scissors

Type of Activity: individual or pair

Language Development: listening, speaking, graphical literacy

INS Questions: 29, 30, 31 (see page 35)

Level: literacy, beginning, multilevel

Directions: See Using Bingo, pages 3–4.

Prelistening Map Activity. Using the United States map on handout 1, distinguish between the Northern and Southern states in the Civil War. Have students shade in the Southern states and put lines through the Northern states.

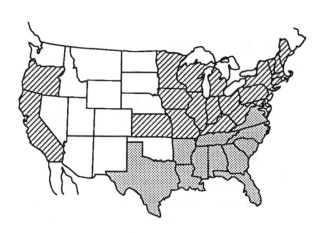

Ideas for Cues. The matchups on Matchups: The Civil War, handout 43, correspond to the pictures on Bingo: The Civil War. Use either the terms on the left side of the matchups or the definitions on the right for bingo cues.

43 MATCHUPS: THE CIVIL WAR

Materials: handout 43, scissors

Type of Activity: whole class

Language Development: listening, speaking, reading

INS Questions: 29, 30, 31 (see page 35)

Level: literacy, beginning, intermediate, multilevel

Directions: (Before doing this activity, you may want to do the Prelistening Map Activity on this page.) See Using Matchups, pages 11-12.

44 STRIP STORY: ABRAHAM LINCOLN AND THE CIVIL WAR

Materials: handout 44, scissors

Type of Activity: whole class or individual

Language Development: listening, speaking, reading, sequencing

INS Questions: 29, 30, 31 (see page 35)

Level: beginning, intermediate

Directions: (Before doing this activity, you may want to do the Prelistening Map Activity on this page.) See Using Strip Stories, p.10.

45 TRIFOLD ACTIVITY

Materials: handouts 1, 45a, 45b; a five dollar bill and a penny

Type of Activity: whole class, individual, and pair

Language Development: prediction, reading, and writing

INS Questions: 29, 30, 31 (see page 35)

Level: beginning, intermediate, multilevel

Directions: Duplicate handouts 1, 45a, and 45b for each student. After duplicating, fold handout 45a on the lines provided so that the picture of the five dollar bill is on top and the reading passage is hidden inside. Distribute copies of the folded handout, five dollar bill side up, and caution students not to turn their papers over or unfold them. Have students predict the subject of the reading by asking the questions next to the picture on the five dollar bill. Then have students turn the paper over, still keeping it folded so that the title is showing. Elicit their ideas about Lincoln and his importance in U.S. history. Then have students unfold the handout and read the passage individually. Distribute copies of handout 1 and ask students to circle all the places where Lincoln lived. (Kentucky, Indiana, Illinois and Washington, D.C.) Have students work in pairs to answer the questions on 45b. Then have students write sentences for the pictures and share them with the class.

Follow-up Activities

Beginning Level:

✪ Discuss the Lincoln Memorial by having students look at the backs of the penny and the five dollar bill. Ask students where the Lincoln Memorial is and if anyone has visited it. Bring in pictures of the Memorial if possible.

✪ Discuss Lincoln's humble beginnings and self-education. Ask students if there are or were leaders with a similar background.

Intermediate Level:

✪ Provide materials for students to do additional research on Lincoln to find out more about his early life, his wife and children, and his presidency. Have them do oral or written reports in class.

46 SKIT: A HOUSE DIVIDED

Materials: handouts 46a, 46b, 46c; table, six chairs, serving bowl, plates, cotton, Dixie flag

Type of Activity: whole class

Language Development: listening, speaking, reading

INS Questions: 29, 30, 31 (see page 35)

Level: intermediate, multilevel

Directions: See Using Skits, pages 12-13.

Follow-up Activities

✪ Class Discussion.

- Discuss how students feel about slavery and the division between North and South. Do they feel that one side was right?

- Ask students if their native countries have had civil wars. When were they? What were the causes and outcomes?

✪ Cause-Effect Composition.
  Have students write a composition about the causes of the Civil War.

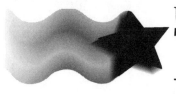

UNIT 8
Twentieth-Century U.S.A.

 47 INFORMATION GAP: TWENTIETH-CENTURY TIME LINE

Materials: handouts 47a, 47b, 47c (On handouts 47a and 47b, write the name of the current President and the year he/she was elected on the lines at the right end of the time line before duplicating. On handout 47c, write only the year of the last presidential election on the line at the right end of the handout before duplicating.)

Type of Activity: pair

Language Development: listening, speaking, graphical literacy

INS Questions: 32, 33, 34, 51, 72, 79 (see pages 35–37)

Level: intermediate

Directions: Use the time line on handout 47a to prepare students for this information gap activity. Discuss each historical event. Ask students which of these events they learned about in their native countries. Were students' native countries involved in any of these events? How?

Guide students in reading the time line by asking *wh-* questions (for example, "What happened in 1920?" "When was the United Nations established?").

Distribute handouts 47b and 47c to each pair of students. Then have them complete their time lines only by asking each other questions; students should never see their partners' papers.

Follow-up Activity

⭐ Provide reference materials and have students (individually or in small groups) prepare an oral or written report on one of the events shown in the time line.

 48 CHART READING: THE U.S. IN CONFLICT— TWENTIETH CENTURY

Materials: handouts 48a, 48b

Type of Activity: small group or individual

Language Development: graphical literacy, scanning

INS Questions: 32, 34 (see page 35)

Level: intermediate

Directions: Using the chart on handout 48a, discuss U.S. involvement in these wars. Ask students if their countries were involved in any of them. (Use the world map on handout 12a to aid class discussion.)

Explain column headings and guide students in scanning the chart for specific information. Then have students work together in groups of four to six (or individually) to answer the questions on handout 48b.

Answers:

1. Vietnam war

2. The United States opposed unrestricted submarine warfare by Germany.

3. the Allies (United States, England, France, Russia, and others)

4. United States and South Korea vs.
   North Korea and China

5. Japan

6. 1941

7. Germany, Italy, and Japan (Axis Powers)

8. England, Russia, France, and the United States

9. World War II

10. 1950-1953

Follow-up Activities

⭐ Discuss military, political, and economic relations between the United States and the Soviet Union before its break-up. Discuss the Cold War, glasnost, perestroika, and Solidarity.

⭐ Have students choose one of the wars and do an oral or written report.

⭐ Have students work in pairs and ask each other review questions about the chart.

49 CHRONOLOGICAL LINEUP

Materials: handout 49 (write the name of the current president on the last strip before duplicating), scissors

Type of Activity: whole class

Language Development: listening, speaking, reading

INS Questions: general review (see pages 34–39)

Level: beginning, intermediate

Directions: Duplicate enough copies of the handout so that each student will receive one sentence (if necessary, divide the class into two groups or have students work in pairs). Cut the strips and put them in a box. Have each student pick a strip. Then have students, working together as a group, line up in chronological order according to their events. After students have lined up, have each one read his or her strip to the class. Alternatively, duplicate and cut one copy of the handout for each student and have students work individually.

Follow-up Activities

⭐ Have students give additional facts about these events in history.

⭐ Elicit from students other important events to add to the human time line.

50 BINGO: REVIEW OF NUMBERS AND DATES

Materials: handout 50

Type of Activity: individual or pair

Language Development: listening, speaking

INS Questions: 2, 4, 5, 6, 9, 10, 18, 20, 21, 24, 37, 39, 44, 51, 62, 63, 64, 66, 67, 92 (see pages 34–38)

Level: literacy, beginning, intermediate, multilevel

Directions: Before completing this activity, read Using Bingo, pages 3–4.

Ideas for Cues

1. How many Supreme Court justices are there? (9)

2. What is the minimum voting age in the United States? (18)

3. How many senators are from _____ (your state)? (2)

4. For how many years do we elect each senator? (6)

5. What is the date of Independence Day? (July 4, 1776)
   or
   When was the Declaration of Independence signed? (July 4, 1776)

6. How many changes or amendments are there to the Constitution? (26)

7. How many senators are there in Congress? (100)

8. How many representatives are there in Congress? (435)

9. How many branches are there in our government? (3)

10. How many stars are on the flag? (50)
   or
   How many states are there in the Union? (50)

11. In what year was the Constitution written? (1787)

12. How many stripes are in the flag? (13)
   or
   How many colonies or states were there in 1776? (13)

Follow-up Activities

 Cut up one or two copies of handout 50 and put the pieces into a box. Have a student pick an item and tell what significance it has. (If a student picks "100," for example, she or he could say, "There are one hundred senators in Congress.") Ask the rest of the class if they agree or disagree with the student's comment. Continue with another student.

 Write the review numbers and dates on the board and have students write a sentence for each one.

51 ELIMINATION EXERCISE

Materials: handout 51

Type of Activity: small group or individual

Language Development: listening, speaking, reading

INS Questions: general review (see pages 34–39)

Level: beginning, intermediate, multilevel

Directions: Put students in small groups of four to six and give each student a copy of handout 51. Have students work toward group consensus as they decide which words

to eliminate. Correct the exercise and have students justify their answers.

Intermediate Level. Have students add another appropriate word for each list and name the category on the line provided.

Follow-up Activity

 Have students write one sentence for each set of words (for example: The three branches of government are the legislative, executive, and judicial.).

Answers:
These words should be eliminated.

1. municipal
2. King
3. Jamestown
4. black
5. justices
6. Revolutionary War
7. *Mayflower*
8. Senate
9. Philadelphia
10. Congress
11. Declaration of Independence
12. six-year term
13. executive
14. Franklin
15. voting
16. citizen 9+ years

52 PATRIOTS PUZZLE

Materials: handout 52

Type of Activity: individual or pair

Language Development: reading, writing

INS Questions: 15, 17, 26, 28, 29, 33 (see pages 34–35)

Level: beginning, intermediate

Directions: Review the meaning of the word *patriot*. Elicit from students names of famous patriots throughout American history. Be sure students associate each name with an accomplishment or period of history.

Beginning Level. Leave handout 52 intact. Assist students as necessary.

Intermediate Level. Before duplicating, fold or cut off the word bank at the bottom of the handout.

Follow-up Activities

⭐ Review the patriots in the puzzle to see if students can supply additional facts about these famous Americans.

⭐ Have students (individually or in small groups) research one of these people and then do an oral and/or written report to share with the class.

Answers:

Patrick Henry
Thomas Jefferson
Betsy Ross
Harriet Tubman
Abraham Lincoln
George Washington
Martin Luther King, Jr.
Francis Scott Key

53 WHO AM I?

Materials: handout 53 (Before duplicating handout 53, fill in the names of current government leaders in the blanks provided.), scissors, tape or straight pins

Type of Activity: whole class or small group

Language Development: listening, speaking, reading

INS Questions: general review (see pages 34–39)

Level: beginning, intermediate

Directions: Cut the strips with one name on each strip. Choose names of famous Americans your students have already studied. Tape or pin one name on each student's back. Do *not* allow the students to see the names on their own strips. Have them ask each other yes/no questions to find out their new identities (for example, "Am I living?" "Am I a President?"). The first student to find out who he or she is wins a prize! Play can continue until all students know who they are. The content of the game may be limited to a certain category of names (current government leaders, Presidents, and so on). The game can also be played in small groups, each having the same names.

Follow-up Activity

⭐ Have each student tell the class one important fact about the famous American he or she is supposed to be.

Immigration and Naturalization Service (INS) Questions

These questions are typical of those used by the INS during the interview for naturalization. The questions are organized into content categories for ease in review.

Applicants will be expected to answer aloud a limited number of the questions when asked by the INS examiner. (For self-study, students can move a sheet of paper down the page, uncovering the answer after reading each question.) In addition, applicants will be asked to read aloud and write from dictation a few of the thirty statements from the INS Reading/Writing Test.

The one hundred Oral Interview Questions and Answers are recorded on *The Uncle Sam Activity Tape* followed by thirty statements for dictation practice. Fifteen reworded questions are also included on the tape.

U.S. FLAG

INS Oral Interview

1. What are the colors of the American flag?
   (red, white, and blue)

2. How many stars are there on the flag?
   (fifty)

3. What color are the stars on the flag?
   (white)

4. What do the stars on the flag mean?
   (one for each state in the Union)

5. How many states are in the Union?
   (fifty)

6. How many states are in the United States?
   (fifty)

7. What are the forty-ninth and fiftieth states in the Union?
   (Hawaii and Alaska)

8. What color are the stripes on the flag?
   (red and white)

9. How many stripes are there on the flag?
   (thirteen)

10. What do the stripes on the flag mean?
    (They represent the original thirteen states.)

U.S. HISTORY

INS Oral Interview

Pilgrims

11. Why did the Pilgrims come to America?
    (for religious freedom)

12. Who helped the Pilgrims in America?
    (the American Indians/Native Americans)

13. What is the name of the ship that brought the Pilgrims to America?
    (the *Mayflower*)

14. What holiday was celebrated for the first time by the American colonists?
    (Thanksgiving)

Independence

15. Who said, "Give me liberty or give me death"?
    (Patrick Henry)

16. What country did we fight during the Revolutionary War?
    (England)

17. Who was the main writer of the Declaration of Independence?
    (Thomas Jefferson)

18. When was the Declaration of Independence adopted?
    (July 4, 1776)

19. What is the basic belief of the Declaration of Independence?
(that all men are created equal)

20. What is the Fourth of July?
(Independence Day)

21. What is the date of Independence Day?
(July 4)

22. Independence from whom?
(England)

23. Can you name the thirteen original states?
(Connecticut, New Hampshire, New York, New Jersey, Massachusetts, Pennsylvania, Delaware, Virginia, North Carolina, South Carolina, Georgia, Rhode Island, Maryland)

24. What were the thirteen original states in the United States called?
(colonies)

25. Which President is called The Father of Our Country?
(George Washington)

26. Which President was the first commander in chief of the U.S. military?
(George Washington)

27. What is the national anthem of the United States?
("The Star-Spangled Banner")

28. Who wrote "The Star-Spangled Banner"?
(Francis Scott Key)

LINCOLN AND THE CIVIL WAR

29. Who was the President during the Civil War?
(Abraham Lincoln)

30. What did the Emancipation Proclamation do?
(freed many slaves)

31. Which President freed the slaves?
(Abraham Lincoln)

TWENTIETH-CENTURY HISTORY

32. Name one purpose of the United Nations.
(for countries to discuss and try to resolve world problems; to provide economic aid to many countries)

33. Who was Martin Luther King, Jr.?
(a civil rights leader)

34. Which countries were our enemies during World War II?
(Germany, Italy, Japan)

THE CONSTITUTION

INS Oral Interview

35. What is the supreme law of the United States?
(the Constitution)

36. What is the Constitution?
(the supreme law of the land)

37. In what year was the Constitution written?
(1787)

38. What is the introduction to the Constitution called?
(the Preamble)

39. How many branches are there in our government?
(three)

40. What are the three branches of our government?
(legislative, executive, and judiciary)

41. What kind of government does the United States have?
(republican)

42. Can the Constitution be changed?
(yes)

43. What do we call a change to the Constitution?
(an amendment)

44. How many changes or amendments are there to the Constitution?
(twenty-six)

45. What are the first ten amendments to the Constitution called?
(the Bill of Rights)

46. What is the Bill of Rights?
(the first ten amendments to the Constitution)

47. Whose rights are guaranteed by the Constitution and the Bill of Rights?
(everyone's—citizens and noncitizens living in the United States)

48. Name one right guaranteed by the first amendment.
(freedom of speech, freedom of the press, freedom of religion, right to have peaceable assembly, and right to request change of the government)

49. Where does freedom of speech come from?
(the Bill of Rights)

50. Name three rights or freedoms guaranteed by the Bill of Rights.

1. The right of freedom of speech, press, religion, peaceable assembly, and requesting change of government.

2. The right to bear arms (the right to have weapons or own a gun, though subject to certain regulations)

3. The government may not quarter, or house, soldiers in people's homes during peacetime without the people's consent.

4. The government may not search or take a person's property without a warrant.

5. A person may not be tried twice for the same crime and does not have to testify against himself or herself.

6. A person charged with a crime still has some rights, such as the right to a trial and to have a lawyer.

7. The right to a trial by jury in most cases.

8. Protects people against excessive or unreasonable fines or cruel and unusual punishment.

9. The people have rights other than those mentioned in the Constitution.

10. Any power not given to the federal government by the Constitution is a power of either the state or the people.

51. What is the minimum voting age in the United States?
(eighteen)

52. Name one benefit of being a citizen of the United States.
(obtain federal government jobs, travel with a U.S. passport, petition for close relatives to come to the United States to live)

53. What is the most important right granted to U.S. citizens?
(the right to vote)

LEGISLATIVE BRANCH

INS Oral Interview

54. What is the legislative branch of our government?
(Congress)

55. What is Congress?
(the Senate and the House of Representatives)

56. Where does Congress meet?
(in the Capitol in Washington, D.C.)

57. What is the United States Capitol?
(the place where Congress meets)

58. What are the duties of Congress?
(to make laws)

59. Who makes the laws in the United States?
(Congress)

60. Who has the power to declare war?
(Congress)

61. Who elects Congress?
(the people)

62. How many senators are there in Congress?
(one hundred)

63. Why are there one hundred senators in the Senate?
(two from each state)

64. For how long do we elect each senator?
(six years)

65. How many times may a senator be reelected?
(There is no limit.)

66. Can you name the two senators from your state?
(varies)

67. How many representatives are there in Congress?
(435)

68. For how long do we elect the representatives?
(two years)

69. How many times may a Congressman or Congresswoman be reelected?
(There is no limit.)

70. What are the two major political parties in the U.S. today?
(Democrats and Republicans)

EXECUTIVE BRANCH

INS Oral Interview

71. What is the executive branch of our government?
(the President, cabinet, and departments under the cabinet members)

72. Who is the President of the United States today?
(varies)

73. Who is the Vice President of the United States today?
(varies)

74. What is the name of the President's official home?
(the White House)

75. What is the White House?
(the President's official home)

76. Where is the White House located?
(Washington, D.C.—1600 Pennsylvania Avenue, NW)

77. Who elects the President of the United States?
(the electoral college)

78. For how long do we elect the President?
(four years)

79. How many terms can a President serve?
(two)

80. In what month do we vote for the President?
(November)

81. In what month is the new President inaugurated?
(January)

82. According to the Constitution, a person must meet certain requirements to be eligible to become President. Name one of the requirements.
(must be a natural-born citizen of the United States; must be at least thirty-five years old by the time he or she will serve; must have lived in the United States for at least fourteen years)

83. Who becomes President of the United States if the President should die?
(the Vice President)

84. Who becomes President of the United States if the President and the Vice President should die?
(the Speaker of the House of Representatives)

85. Who signs bills into law?
(the President)

86. Who is the commander in chief of the U.S. military?
(the President)

87. What special group advises the President?
(the Cabinet)

88. Who was the first President of the United States?
(George Washington)

JUDICIAL BRANCH

INS Oral Interview

89. What is the judicial branch of our government?
(the Supreme Court and other Federal courts)

90. What is the highest court in the United States?
(the Supreme Court)

91. What are the duties of the Supreme Court?
(to interpret laws)

92. How many Supreme Court justices are there?
(nine)

93. Who selects the Supreme Court justices?
(They are appointed by the President.)

94. Who is the chief justice of the Supreme Court?
(William Rehnquist)

STATE AND LOCAL GOVERNMENT

INS Oral Interview

95. What is the head executive of a state government called?
(governor)

96. Who is the current governor of your state?
(varies)

97. What is the capital of your state?
(varies)

98. What is the head executive of a city government called?
(mayor)

99. Who is the head of your local government?
(varies)

MISCELLANEOUS

100. What Immigration and Naturalization Service form is used to apply to become a naturalized citizen?
(Form N-400, "Application to File Petition for Naturalization")

INS READING/WRITING TEST

The Flag

1. The American flag is red, white, and blue.
2. The American flag has thirteen stripes.
3. The American flag has fifty stars.
4. The stars of the American flag are white.
5. The stars represent the fifty states in the Union.
6. The stripes of the American flag are red and white.

The President

7. The President lives in Washington, D.C.
8. The President lives in the White House.
9. The White House is in Washington, D.C.
10. The President has the power of veto.
11. The President is elected every four years.
12. The President signs bills into law.
13. The President must be born in the United States.
14. The President must be an American citizen.

Congress

15. Congress is part of the American government.
16. Congress meets in Washington, D.C.
17. Congress passes laws in the United States.
18. Only Congress can declare war.
19. The House and the Senate are part of Congress.
20. A Senator is elected for six years.

America

21. America is the land of the free.

22. America is the home of the brave.

23. There are fifty states in America.

Rights of the People

24. The people have a voice in the government.

25. Citizens have the right to vote.

26. People vote for the President in November.

27. Many people come to America for freedom.

28. People in America have the right to freedom.

29. Many people have died for freedom.

Three Branches of Government

30. There are three branches of government.

Song Lyrics

AMERICA THE BEAUTIFUL

Oh beautiful for spacious skies,
For amber waves of grain,
For purple mountain majesties
Above the fruited plain.
America! America!
God shed His grace on thee.
And crown thy good with brotherhood
From sea to shining sea.
Oh beautiful for pilgrim feet
Whose stern, impassioned stress
A thoroughfare for freedom beat
Across the wilderness.
America! America!
God mend thine every flaw.
Confirm thy soul in self control,
Thy liberty in law.

THIS LAND IS YOUR LAND

by Woody Guthrie

This land is your land, this land is my
    land
From California to the New York island,
From the redwood forest to the Gulf
    Stream waters;
This land was made for you and me.
As I went walking that ribbon of highway
I saw above me that endless skyway;
I saw below me that golden valley;
This land was made for you and me.
This land is your land, this land is my
    land
From California to the New York island,
From the redwood forest to the Gulf
    Stream waters;
This land was made for you and me.
I roamed and rambled, and I followed my
    footsteps
To the sparkling sands of her diamond
    deserts;

And all around me a voice was sounding:
This land was made for you and me.
This land is your land, this land is my
    land
From California to the New York island,
From the redwood forest to the Gulf
    Stream waters;
This land was made for you and me.
The sun came shining, and I was strolling,
And the wheat fields waving and the dust
    clouds rolling,
As the fog was lifting a voice was calling:
This land was made for you and me.
This land is your land, this land is my
    land
From California to the New York island,
From the redwood forest to the Gulf
    Stream waters;
This land was made for you and me.

MY COUNTRY 'TIS OF THEE

My country 'tis of thee
Sweet land of liberty
Of thee I sing.
Land where my fathers died,
Land of the Pilgrims' pride,
From every mountain side
Let freedom ring.
Let music swell the breeze
And ring from all the trees
Sweet freedom's song.
Let mortal tongues awake,
Let all that breathe partake,
Let rocks their silence break,
The sound prolong.

THE STAR-SPANGLED BANNER

Oh say, can you see,
by the dawn's early light,
What so proudly we hailed
at the twilight's last gleaming.
Whose broad stripes and bright stars
through the perilous fight,
O'er the ramparts we watched
were so gallantly streaming;
And the rocket's red glare,
the bombs bursting in air,
Gave proof through the night
that our flag was still there.
Oh say, does that star-spangled
banner yet wave
O'er the land of the free
and the home of the brave?
Oh thus be it ever
when free men shall stand
Between their loved homes
and the war's desolation!
Blest with victory and peace,
may the heaven rescued land
Praise the Power that hath made
and preserved us a nation.
Then conquer we must,
when our cause it is just,
And this be our motto:
"In God is our trust."
And the star-spangled banner
in triumph shall wave
O'er the land of the free
and the home of the brave.

ABRAHAM, MARTIN, AND JOHN

Anybody here seen my old friend
    Abraham?
Can you tell me where he's gone?
He freed a lot of people
But it seems the good they die young.
You know, I just look around and he's
    gone.

Anybody here seen my old friend John?
Can you tell me where's gone?
He freed a lot of people
But it seems the good they die young.
I just look around and he's gone.
Anybody here seen my old friend Martin?
Can you tell me where he's gone?
He freed a lot of people
But it seems the good they die young.
I just look around and he's gone.
Didn't you love the things that they stood
    for?
Didn't they try to find some good for you
    and me?
And we'll be free some day soon.
It's gonna be one day.
Anybody here seen my old friend Bobby?
Can you tell me where he's gone?
I thought I saw him walking up over the
    hill
With Abraham, Martin, and John.

AMERICAN WOMEN: A TRIBUTE TO SUSAN B. ANTHONY, HARRIET TUBMAN, AND ROSA PARKS

Susan was a suffragette
Who thought that women had the right to
    vote.
Susan was a suffragette
Who thought that women had the right to
    vote.
She was an American woman who made
    this country strong.
She was an American woman who made
    this country strong.
Harriet risked her life
To lead fellow slaves to freedom.
Harriet risked her life
To lead fellow slaves to freedom.
She was an American woman who made
    this country strong.

She was an American woman who made
　　this country strong.
Rosa wouldn't give in
Just because of the shade of her skin.
Rosa wouldn't give in
Just because of the shade of her skin.
She was an American woman who made
　　this country strong.
She was an American woman who made
　　this country strong.
Susan, Harriet, and Rosa
Raised their voices for what they
　　believed.
Susan, Harriet, and Rosa
Raised their voices for what they
　　believed.
These were American women who made
　　this country strong.
These were American women who made
　　this country strong.
They let freedom ring, let freedom ring,
Let freedom ring, ring for us all.
Let freedom ring, let freedom ring,
Let freedom ring, ring for us all.
Ring for us all.

Handouts

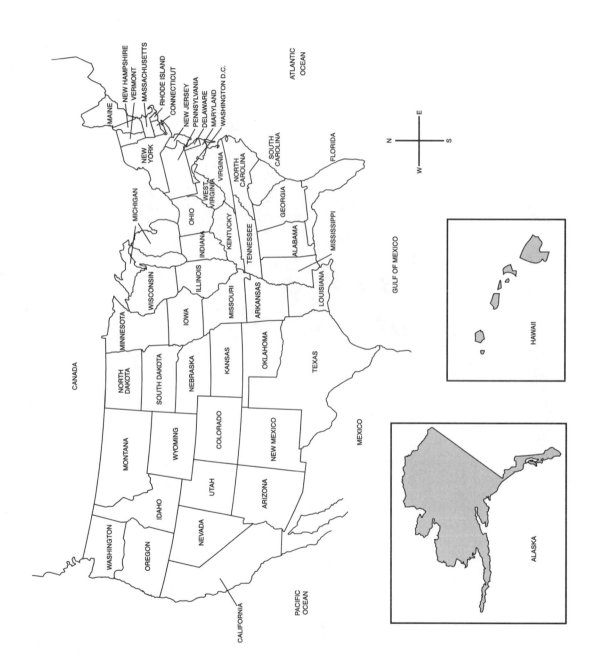

Information Gap: Map of the U.S.A.

Partner One

Directions: Ask your partner where these places are and write their names on your map.
Do *not* look at your partner's map.

Canada	**California**	**Alaska**
Atlantic Ocean	**Rhode Island**	**Florida**

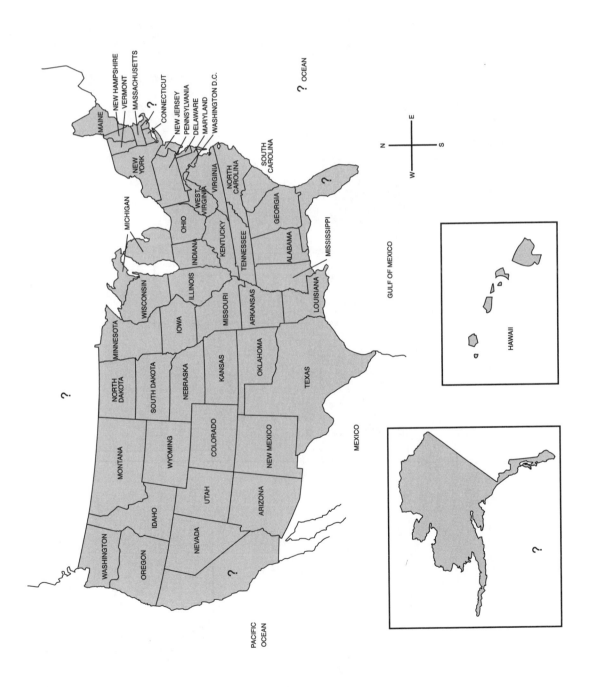

45

Information Gap: Map of the U.S.A.

Partner Two

Directions: Ask your partner where these places are and write their names on your map. Do *not* look at your partner's map.

Mexico	Texas	Hawaii
Pacific Ocean	New York	Virginia

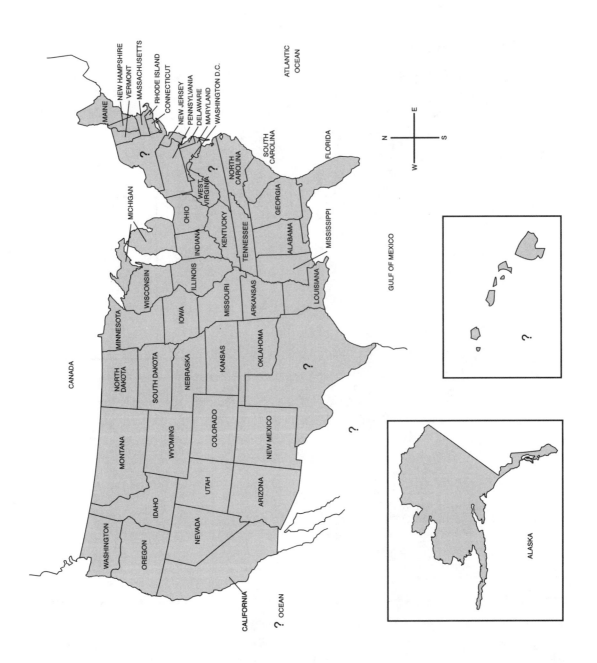

Bingo: America
United States Map

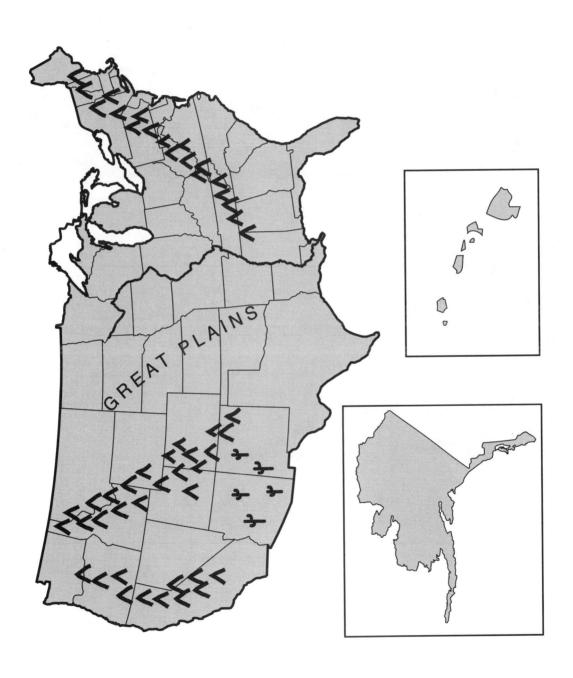

Directions: Cut and paste in random order onto the bingo grid (handout 3c).

BINGO

Word Cues: "America the Beautiful"

Beautiful	**Skies**
Grain	**Purple**
Mountain	**Plain**
America	**Sea**

Modified Cloze Listening: "America the Beautiful"

Directions: Circle the word you hear.

1. Oh beautiful | in / for | spacious skies

2. For amber waves | for / of | grain,

3. For | green / purple | mountain majesties

4. Above the fruited | grain / plain |

5. America! | the Beautiful! / America! |

6. God shed His grace | on / to | thee.

7. And crown thy good with | sisterhood / brotherhood |

8. | For / From | sea to shining sea.

Cloze Listening: "America the Beautiful"

Beginning Level

AMERICA THE BEAUTIFUL

Oh _____ for spacious skies,

For amber waves of _____,

For _____ mountain majesties

Above _____ fruited plain.

America! _____

God shed His grace _____ thee.

And crown thy good _____ brotherhood

From sea to shining _____.

Intermediate Level

AMERICA THE BEAUTIFUL

Oh _____ for spacious _____,

For amber waves _____ grain,

For _____ _____ majesties

Above _____ fruited plain.

_____ America!

God shed _____ grace _____ thee.

_____ crown thy _____

_____ brotherhood

_____ sea _____ shining _____.

Word Cues: "This Land Is Your Land" (Verse 1)

Land	**California**
New York	**Island**
Forest	**Waters**
You	**Me**

Word Cues: "This Land Is Your Land" (Verses 2 and 3)

Walking	**Highway**
Skyway	**Valley**
Footsteps	**Sands**
Deserts	**Voice**

Cloze Listening: "This Land Is Your Land"

Directions: Listen to the song. Write the missing words.

THIS LAND IS YOUR LAND

by Woody Guthrie

Beginning/Intermediate Levels

This land is _____ land, this land is _____ land

_____ California _____ the New York island,

_____ the redwood forest _____ the Gulf Stream waters;

This land was made _____ you and me.

_____ I went walking that ribbon _____ highway

I saw _____ me that endless skyway;

I saw _____ me that golden valley;

This land was made _____ you and me.

This land is _____ land, this land is _____ land

_____ California _____ the New York island,

_____ the redwood forest _____ the Gulf Stream waters;

This land was made _____ you and me.

Intermediate Level

I roamed and rambled, and I followed my footsteps

_____ the sparkling sands _____ her diamond deserts;

And all _____ me a voice was sounding:

This land was made _____ you and me.

This land is _____ land, this land is _____ land

_____ California _____ the New York island,

_____ the redwood forest _____ the Gulf Stream waters;

This land was made _____ you and me.

The American Flag

The American Flag in Everyday Life

Cloze: The Pledge of Allegiance

I PLEDGE ALLEGIANCE _____ THE FLAG

_____ THE UNITED STATES _____ AMERICA

AND _____ THE REPUBLIC _____ WHICH

IT STANDS, ONE NATION, _____ GOD, INDIVISIBLE,

_____ LIBERTY AND JUSTICE _____ ALL.

Picture Sequencing Activity:
Christopher Columbus—World Map

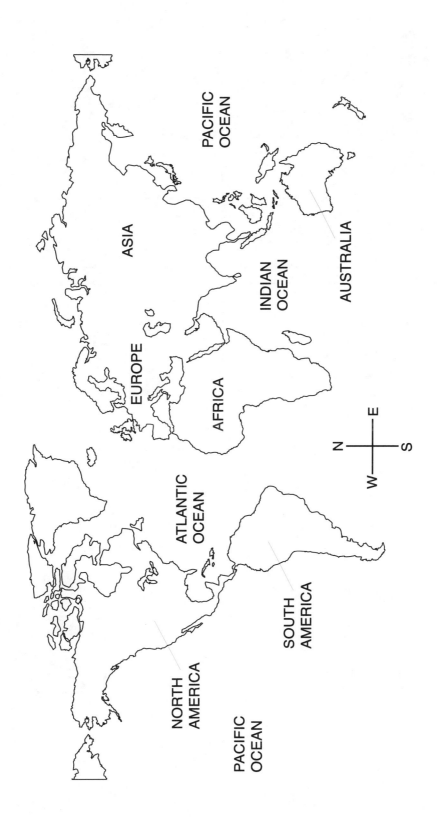

12b Picture Sequencing Activity: Christopher Columbus

Strip Story: Christopher Columbus and the New World

Christopher Columbus and the New World

Christopher Columbus was a sailor from Italy.

In his time, people went to Asia by land to buy silk and spices.

By land, the trip to Asia was long and difficult.

Columbus thought there was an easier way to reach Asia.

He thought he could cross the Atlantic Ocean to get to Asia.

So he asked the king and queen of Spain for help.

They gave him three ships and some sailors.

In 1492, Columbus sailed west from Spain in these three ships.

Columbus sailed for ten weeks.

When he reached land, he thought he was in India.

For this reason, he called the people he saw "Indians."

But he was not in India; he had discovered a new land.

This new land was called the "New World."

Today the New World is known as North, Central, and South America.

Directions: Cut and paste in random order onto the bingo grid (handout 3c).

Matchups: Early Settlers

England	was the native country of the Pilgrims and the Jamestown traders.
Jamestown	was the first permanent English colony in America (1607).
Tobacco	was a plant grown and traded by the Jamestown settlers.
The Pilgrims	were people who came to America for religious freedom.
Religious freedom	is the right to worship as one chooses.
The *Mayflower*	was the Pilgrims' ship.
The Mayflower Compact	was the Pilgrims' law.
Plymouth	was the Massachusetts colony of the Pilgrims (1620).
William Bradford	was the governor of Plymouth.
Native Americans	were Indians, who helped the Pilgrims plant corn.
Turkey, corn, and squash	were foods eaten at the first Thanksgiving.
Thanksgiving	is the holiday feast started by the Pilgrims and the Indians.

A skit for ten actors about the first Thanksgiving.

Scene 1. Sitting around a table

NARRATOR: Some people in England were practicing their own religion. Their neighbors were angry because these Pilgrims did not belong to the Church of England.

WILLIAM BREWSTER: I worship God in my own way. No one will force me to join the Church of England.

PILGRIM 1: I agree. We want religious freedom.

REV. JOHN ROBINSON: *(holding cross)* My people, God will show us the way.

PILGRIM 1: But the neighbors punish us. We want to worship in peace.

BREWSTER: Let's go to Holland. They have many different religions there. I'll sell my land for money for our trip.

Scene 2. Standing outside their church

NARRATOR: Brewster sold his land, and they moved to Holland. But the Pilgrims were not happy with Dutch customs. Some members stayed in Holland, but others returned to England.

PILGRIM 1: I'm afraid our church is still in danger.

BREWSTER: I have read Captain John Smith's *Description of New England.* Let's go to the New World!

EDWIN SANDYS: Gentlemen, Virginia is paradise. It's a land of rich soil. Tobacco trade is very successful.

PILGRIM 2: Money is not important to us. We only want religious freedom.

ROBINSON: Let's leave soon. We have the king's permission.

Scene 3. At sea and sitting at a table

NARRATOR: The Pilgrims finally left for the New World in September of 1620. They sailed on the *Mayflower* for many weeks. Because winter was coming, they decided to land at Plymouth, Massachusetts.

PILGRIM 2: Tomorrow we land.

Skit: The Pilgrims in America (continued)

PILGRIM 3: Because we're not in Virginia, let's write laws for our colony.
(*pulls out a roll of paper and a pen*)

PILGRIM 2: (*pointing to paper*) Write down that we are loyal to King James.

BREWSTER: (*pointing to paper*) And write that we will vote about government and laws.

PILGRIM 3: (*writing*) We should also have majority rule.

PILGRIM 2: Let's call our law the Mayflower Compact.

Scene 4. Standing on land

NARRATOR: The next day, December 21, the Pilgrims landed in Plymouth. Life was very difficult, and many died before spring. William Bradford was elected the new governor.

WILLIAM BRADFORD: We must work together on our houses and farms.

PILGRIM 3: Governor, this Indian wants to help us. (*points to Squanto*)

SQUANTO: The river has many fish. (*points to river*) We plant corn for food. (*kneels, digs, and puts in corn kernels*)

PILGRIM 4: Our Indian friend Squanto will help us. He told his people we are friends. They won't hurt us.

PILGRIM 2: Good! God is watching over us.

NARRATOR: Time passed. The corn grew tall. The Pilgrims learned to live in a new land.

BRADFORD: It's time to harvest the corn. Let's have a feast of Thanksgiving.

PILGRIM 4: We can eat wild turkey, corn, berries, and nuts.

BRADFORD: Invite the Indians for food and friendship. Let's give thanks for life in the New World!

The First Thanksgiving

The Pilgrims were unhappy in England.

They wanted religious freedom, but their king said no.

So in 1620 they decided to go to America.

They traveled to America on a large ship.

It was called the Mayflower.

The Mayflower landed at Plymouth, Massachusetts, in winter.

Life in Plymouth was difficult for the Pilgrims.

Many died from hunger and the cold weather.

The others met Indians who helped them plant corn.

After the first harvest, they made a big dinner.

They invited the Indians to eat with them.

This was the first Thanksgiving.

Now we celebrate Thanksgiving every November too.

Information Gap: Map of the Thirteen Colonies

Information Gap: Map of the Thirteen Colonies

Partner One

Directions: Ask your partner where these colonies are and write their names on your map. Do *not* look at your partner's map.

Georgia	Massachusetts
New Jersey	**Delaware**

Information Gap: Map of the Thirteen Colonies

Partner Two

Directions: Ask your partner where these colonies are and write their names on your map. Do *not* look at your partner's map.

North Carolina	Virginia
Connecticut	New York

Skit: Let Freedom Ring!

A skit about the Declaration of Independence with eleven actors.

On the back of the two-dollar bill is a copy of a famous painting of the signing of the Declaration of Independence. The tall man standing in front of the desk is Thomas Jefferson. Benjamin Franklin stands to the right of Jefferson.

Scene 1. Standing in a small group

NARRATOR: The Revolutionary War began in 1775. The colonies were fighting England. It is now 1776. Leaders from the thirteen colonies are meeting at the Second Continental Congress in Independence Hall, Philadelphia.

LEADER 1: We must be loyal to England. We're part of her!

LEADER 2: No! We are at war with England. Now's the time to break free!

THOMAS PAINE: That's right! *We* must lead our country *(points to other leaders and himself)*, not King George!

LEADER 1: No. *(shakes head)* England is our mother country. George III is our king.

LEADER 2: Down with the king! Fight for freedom now!

LEADER 3: Separation is dangerous. Be true to England.

PAINE and LEADER 2: *(shouting)* No!

LEADER 1 and LEADER 3: Yes! *(show anger)*

JOHN ADAMS: Please, please. We can't argue. The colonies must be united. We have to agree on what to tell King George.

LEADER 4: The message must be clear. We want to be free and independent states!

Scene 2. Sitting at a table

NARRATOR: After much discussion, the leaders finally agreed. They chose Thomas Jefferson, Roger Sherman, Robert Livingston, Benjamin Franklin, and John Adams to write a document. It was called the Declaration of Independence.

BENJAMIN FRANKLIN: Let's write down our complaints against the king.

ROBERT LIVINGSTON: Taxation without representation!

ADAMS: Putting soldiers in our houses without our permission!

ROGER SHERMAN: Cutting off our trade with other countries!

THOMAS JEFFERSON: England's laws are unfair.

SHERMAN: Tell the king we have decided to become thirteen united states.

LIVINGSTON: Who should write our declaration?

FRANKLIN: Let Thomas Jefferson do it.

JEFFERSON: Why me?

FRANKLIN: You write so well, Thomas. Your words have power. *(All walk away, and Jefferson is left alone sitting and writing.)*

Scene 3. Standing and talking

NARRATOR: And so Jefferson worked long and hard to express their ideas. His mind and heart chose the right words.

JEFFERSON: *(walking toward the others)* Gentlemen, the declaration is finished. It states our basic belief that all men are created equal.

JOHN HANCOCK: *(reaching for the paper)* What else does it say?

JEFFERSON: *(reading)* All people have the right to life, liberty, and the pursuit of happiness.

HANCOCK: *(reading)* It also says the colonies are free and independent states.

ADAMS: Now we can write our own laws and choose our own leaders.

LIVINGSTON: We must all sign the declaration.

JEFFERSON: Yes. With this document, we pledge to each other our lives.

FRANKLIN: We must all hang together *(joins hands with others)*, or most assuredly we will all hang separately. *(holds up rope with a noose)*

HANCOCK: *(taking quill pen)* Let me be first! My name will be so big that King George won't need his glasses to read it!

(writes)

ADAMS: This is an important day in history, July 4, 1776.

(Liberty Bell rings out.)

ALL: Let freedom ring!

Scrambled Song: "My Country 'Tis of Thee"

My country 'tis of thee

Sweet land of liberty

Of thee I sing

Land where my fathers died,

Land of the Pilgrims' pride,

From every mountain side

Let freedom ring.

Caret Listening: "My Country 'Tis of Thee"

Directions: Listen to the song. Put a caret (∧) where you see a missing word.

My Country 'Tis of Thee

My country 'tis ∧ thee

Sweet land liberty

Of thee sing.

Land where fathers died,

Land the Pilgrims' pride,

Every mountain side

Let freedom ring.

Strip Story: Francis Scott Key and "The Star-Spangled Banner"

Francis Scott Key and "The Star-Spangled Banner"

The United States fought England in the War of 1812.

One night during this war, the English attacked a fort in Maryland.

They were shooting at the fort from their ships in the harbor.

An American, Francis Scott Key, was watching the battle.

Because it was raining, he couldn't see very well.

So he wasn't sure if the Americans were winning the battle.

The next morning, Key saw the American flag still flying over the fort.

For this reason, he knew that the United States had won the battle.

He was so happy that he wrote a poem about the battle.

This poem became a song know as "The Star-Spangled Banner."

Today "The Star-Spangled Banner" is the national anthem of the United States.

Listening Activity:
"The Star-Spangled Banner"

Directions: Listen to the song. Put a caret (∧) where you see a missing word.

**The Star-Spangled Banner
(The National Anthem)**

Oh say, can ∧ see,

by dawn's early light,

What so proudly hailed

at twilight's gleaming.

Whose broad stripes bright

through perilous fight,

O'er the ramparts watched

were gallantly streaming;

And the rocket's glare,

bombs bursting air,

Gave proof the night

that flag was there.

Oh does star-spangled

banner yet wave

O'er land of free

and home the brave?

—Written by Francis Scott Key in 1814

Skit: We the People

A skit about the writing of the Constitution for eleven actors.

This is a picture of Independence Hall in Philadelphia, Pennsylvania, where the Constitution was written. The Liberty Bell first hung in the tower of Independence Hall.

Scene 1. Standing near the windows

NARRATOR: It is a long, hot summer in 1787. The Constitutional Convention is meeting in Independence Hall. There are fifty-five men from twelve states. Only Rhode Island has not sent a representative.

BENJAMIN FRANKLIN: What power we have!

LEADER 1: Yes. We are building a new government.

WILLIAM S. JOHNSON: *(fanning himself)* The heat is terrible. Can't we open the windows? *(walks to the window)*

JOHN BLAIR: No! The people outside might hear us!

LEADER 1: Remember, these meetings are secret. *(puts index finger on lips)*

JOHNSON: Oh, yes. Say, where's the leader from Rhode Island?

BLAIR: Rhode Island is too independent. It isn't interested in a central government.

LEADER 2: That's right. It still wants to print its own money.

FRANKLIN: Well, we want a strong federal government.

LEADER 1: But one that does not take away the freedom of the people.

JAMES MADISON: These are very important ideas. I'll take notes. *(takes out pen and paper)*

© NTC/Contemporary Publishing Group, Inc.

Scene 2. Standing around the table

NARRATOR: So Madison wrote while they talked. The group asked George Washington to be their leader. Sometimes the men shouted and got angry.

GEORGE WASHINGTON: Gentlemen, please come to order. Let's discuss Congress.
(all sit)

LEADER 2: I believe in representation according to population.

MADISON: So do I. Virginia has a lot of people, and we pay a lot of taxes. So we should have more representatives.

JONATHAN DAYTON: I don't think so. We should have *equal* representation for all states, large and small.

LEADER 3: Yes, like the Articles of Confederation. We all agreed to that.

LEADER 2: No!

DAYTON: Yes. Be fair to the smaller states!

ROGER SHERMAN: Maybe we should have two lawmaking branches.
(shows two fingers)

LEADER 2: Yes, yes. A House of Representatives based on population and . . .

SHERMAN: And a Senate with two senators from each state.

LEADER 3: A great idea. A great compromise!

WASHINGTON: Do we all agree?

ALL: Yes!

WASHINGTON: Now let's talk about the President.

LEADER 4: I don't want a President. He would be like a king.

BLAIR: No, no. *(shakes his head)* I mean a man who is elected.

DAYTON: Yes. We can limit his term.

BLAIR: Yes, say *(pause)* to four years.

LEADER 2: If the people want him longer, they can reelect him.

LEADER 4: As long as he doesn't serve for life.

BLAIR: How about a limit of two terms?

DAYTON: Good idea.

ALL: We agree.

Skit: We the People (continued)

Scene 3. Sitting at a table

NARRATOR: The meetings continued for many weeks. The leaders finished planning the three branches of government.

MADISON: Gentlemen, take a look. *(walks to the table)* I have finished our Constitution.

SHERMAN: *(looking at the paper)* Good! Here are the three branches—legislative, executive, and judicial.

BLAIR: *(also reading)* How about an introduction—a Preamble?

WASHINGTON: Good idea. It will state our purpose in writing a Constitution.

MADISON: *(excited and starting to write)* Let me try . . . *(pause)* We the People of the United States . . .

BLAIR: Did you add that part about changes?

MADISON: Yes. The Constitution can be changed by amendments.

DAYTON: *(holding paper and reading)* Then our document is finished.

WASHINGTON: When nine states approve it, it will become the supreme law of the land.

NARRATOR: Eventually all thirteen states approved the Constitution. George Washington, the president of the Constitutional Convention, was elected first President of the United States.

Bingo: Rights and Duties of Citizens

Directions: Cut and paste in random order onto the bingo grid (handout 3c).

Matchups: Rights and Duties of Citizens

Freedom of speech	is the right to say what you want.
Freedom of the press	is the right to print or publish your opinion.
Freedom of religion	is the right to worship as you want.
Freedom of assembly	is the right to meet in a group peacefully.
Owning a gun	is a right with local restrictions.
Police searching your property	is not allowed without a warrant.
A trial and a lawyer	are rights for someone charged with a crime.
Government jobs	are employment possibilities for citizens.
Bringing relatives to the United States	is a right for citizens with family in other countries.
A U.S. passport	is used by U.S. citizens traveling to other countries.
Voting	is a right and duty for citizens eighteen and older.
Paying taxes	is a duty that pays for government.

Application Activity: The Bill of Rights

The Bill of Rights (Amendments 1–10)

Amendment 1. People have religious freedom; there is no government religion.
People can say or print whatever they want. Groups of people
can meet peacefully. People can request a change in government.

Amendment 2. People can have weapons or own a gun (with restrictions).

Amendment 3. The government cannot make people keep soldiers in their
homes in peacetime.

Amendment 4. The government may not search or take a person's property
without a warrant (court order).

Amendment 5. A person may not be tried twice for the same crime and does not
have to testify against himself or herself.

Amendment 6. A person charged with a crime has the right to a trial and a
lawyer.

Amendment 7. A person charged with a crime usually has the right to a trial by
jury.

Amendment 8. The government cannot charge fines that are excessive (too
high). The government cannot punish people in a cruel or
unusual way.

Amendment 9. People have rights in addition to those listed in the Constitution.

Amendment 10. If the Constitution does not give a power to the federal
government, that power belongs to the state or to the people.

Application Activity: The Bill of Rights (continued)

Directions: Which amendment applies to each of these situations?

Write the number of the amendment on the line.

_____ 1. The Baker family goes to the United Church of God every Sunday.

_____ 2. José Lopez was fined $300 for an illegal left turn.

_____ 3. Maria Hernandez keeps a gun under her bed for protection against thieves.

_____ 4. The neighbors on Eastwood Street are meeting tonight to discuss crime in their community.

_____ 5. The city newspaper published a letter written by Eva Dworski disagreeing with the mayor's ideas about public schools.

_____ 6. The police think Tony Martin is selling drugs. While he is at work, they search his apartment without permission.

_____ 7. Joseph Lee was charged with stealing a car. Because he had no money, the court appointed a lawyer for him.

_____ 8. At the university tonight, Angela Wolf is giving a speech called "Is Communism the Answer?"

Chart Reading: Civil Rights Leaders

ABRAHAM LINCOLN 1809–1865

- Was the 16th President of the United States (1861-1865).

- Believed in equality and freedom for all people.

- Was President during the Civil War.

- Signed the Emancipation Proclamation, freeing many slaves.

- Was assassinated in Washington, D.C., in 1865.

JOHN F. KENNEDY 1917–1963

- Was the 35th President of the United States (1961–1963).

- Believed in equality and freedom for all people.

- Supported the "New Frontier" programs to improve civil rights, housing, and education.

- Started the Peace Corps to help people in other countries.

- Was assassinated in Dallas, Texas, in 1963.

MARTIN LUTHER KING, JR. 1929–1968

- Was a minister.

- Believed in equality and freedom for all people.

- Worked for civil rights for African Americans.

- Was awarded the Nobel Peace Prize in 1964 for using nonviolence to achieve equality.

- Was assassinated in Memphis, Tennessee, in 1968.

Chart Reading: Civil Rights Leaders (continued)

Directions: Look at the chart. Answer the questions.

1. Which leader was President during the Civil War? _____

2. Who was a minister? _____

3. Who started the Peace Corps? _____

4. Which leader was not a president? _____

5. Which leader was assassinated? _____

6. Which leader was assassinated more than a hundred
   years ago? _____

7. What did the "New Frontier" programs do? _____

   _____

8. Why did Martin Luther King, Jr. win the Nobel Prize? _____

   _____

9. Which leader believed in equality and freedom for
   all people? _____

10. For how long was John F. Kennedy President? _____

11. How old was Abraham Lincoln when he was assassinated? _____

12. How old was John F. Kennedy when he was assassinated? _____

13. How old was Martin Luther King, Jr., when he was
    assassinated? _____

14. Which leader is remembered for freeing the slaves? _____

Scrambled Song: Abraham, Martin, and John

Abraham, Martin, and John

● Anybody here seen my old friend Abraham?

● Can you tell me where he's gone?

● He freed a lot of people

● But it seems the good they die young.

● You know, I just look around and he's gone.

▲ Anybody here seen my old friend John?

▲ Can you tell me where he's gone?

▲ He freed a lot of people

▲ But it seems the good they die young.

▲ I just look around and he's gone.

■ Anybody here seen my old friend Martin?

■ Can you tell me where he's gone?

■ He freed a lot of people

■ But it seems the good they die young.

■ I just look around and he's gone.

★ Didn't you love the things that they stood for?

★ Didn't they try to find some good for you and me?

★ And we'll be free some day soon.

★ It's gonna be one day.

◆ Anybody here seen my old friend Bobby?

◆ Can you tell me where he's gone?

◆ I thought I saw him walking up over the hill

◆ With Abraham, Martin, and John.

Handout 30a

SUSAN B. ANTHONY
1820–1906

- She was a suffragette, a person who worked to give women the right to vote.

- She was arrested in 1872 for trying to vote.

- Her work helped prepare for the 19th amendment to the Constitution in 1920. This amendment gave women the right to vote.

HARRIET TUBMAN
1821–1913

- She was an abolitionist, a person who worked to end slavery.

- She was born to slave parents before the Civil War.

- She escaped from slavery to freedom in the North in 1849.

- She returned to the South many times to lead 300 slaves to freedom in the North before the Civil War.

ROSA PARKS
1913–

- She worked for equal rights for African Americans.

- She was arrested in 1955 in Montgomery, Alabama, for not giving her bus seat to a white man.

- Her arrest started the Montgomery Alabama Bus Boycott. For 381 days, African Americans would not ride the buses. Then the Supreme Court decided that seating by race was against the law.

Chart Reading: More Civil Rights Leaders (continued)

Directions: Look at the chart. Answer the questions.

1. What is a suffragette? _____

2. What is an abolitionist? _____

3. Who was a slave? _____

4. Who worked to give women the right to vote? _____

5. Who was arrested? Why? _____

6. Who started the Montgomery Alabama Bus Boycott? _____

7. How long did the boycott last? _____

8. Who was an abolitionist? _____

9. Who led over 300 slaves to freedom before the

   Civil War? _____

10. When was the 19th amendment passed? _____

11. What did the 19th amendment do? _____

12. Which leader believed in freedom and equality for

   all people? _____

Cloze Listening: "American Women: A Tribute to Susan B. Anthony, Harriet Tubman, and Rosa Parks"

Directions: Listen to the song. Write the missing words.

AMERICAN WOMEN: A TRIBUTE TO SUSAN B. ANTHONY, HARRIET TUBMAN, AND ROSA PARKS

Susan was a _____

who thought that women had the _____ to

_____. *(repeat)*

She was an American _____

who made this country _____. *(repeat)*

_____ risked her life

to lead fellow _____ to _____. *(repeat)*

She was an American _____

who made this country _____. *(repeat)*

_____ wouldn't give in

just because of the _____ of her _____. *(repeat)*

She was an American _____

who made this country _____. *(repeat)*

Susan, Harriet, _____ Rosa

raised their _____ for what _____ believed. *(repeat)*

These were American _____

who made this country _____. *(repeat)*

_____ let freedom ring, let freedom ring

Let freedom ring, ring for _____ _____. *(repeat)*

Directions: Complete this chart with the names of the people now in office. Write in the branch of government.

Branches

_____
(branch)

U.S. President

U.S. Vice President

_____
(branch)

Speaker of the House of Representatives

U.S. Senators from Your State

U.S. Representative from Your Congressional District

_____
(branch)

Chief Justice of the Supreme Court

Chart Reading:
The Three Branches of Government

Directions: Read the chart and answer the questions below.

Branch	Legislative		Executive	Judicial
	Congress			The Supreme Court
	Senate	House		
Members	100 senators	435 representatives	President, Vice President (Cabinet and Cabinet Depts.)	9 Supreme Court justices
Terms	6-year term; no limit to terms	2-year term; no limit to terms	4-year term; 2 term limit	appointed for life by the President
Qualifications	at least 30 years old; at least 9 years as a U.S. citizen, lives in the state he/she represents	at least 25 years old; at least 7 years as a U.S. citizen, lives in the state he/she represents	at least 35 years old; natural-born citizen, 14 years of U.S. residence	

1. What are the three branches of government?_____

2. Who is in the executive branch?_____

3. How many members are on the Supreme Court?_____

4. How long does a Supreme Court justice serve?_____

5. How many terms can a senator serve?_____

6. How long must a representative have been a citizen?_____

7. How many terms can a representative serve?_____

8. What is another name for the legislative branch?_____

9. How old must the President be?_____

10. How long must the President have lived in the United States?_____

1.	2	50	435
2.	435	50	100
3.	8	4	6
4.	435	100	200
5.	6	2	4
6.	12	2	
7.	4	13	9
8.	2	4	6
9.	2	4	8
10.	9	13	435

Listening Activity:
The Three Branches of Government

Directions: Listen to the statement. Put an X in the column under the correct branch of government.

Legislative Branch
Congress
(House and Senate)

Executive Branch
The President,
Vice President, and
Cabinet

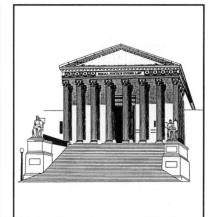

Judicial Branch
Supreme Court
(Nine Justices)

1.

2.

3.

4.

5.

6.

7.

8.

9.

10.

11.

12.

	is the President of the United States.
	is the Vice President of the United States.
The legislative branch	makes the laws.
Representatives	have a two-year term of office.
There are 435	representatives in the House.
There are 100	senators in the Senate.
Senators	have a six-year term of office.
The executive branch	enforces the laws.
The President	can serve only two terms of office.
The cabinet	advises the President.
The judicial branch	interprets the laws.
There are nine	justices on the Supreme Court.
William Rehnquist	is the Chief Justice of the Supreme Court.
The population	determines how many representatives a state has.
The major political parties	are the Democrats and the Republicans.

Bingo: Government Sites and Symbols

Directions: Cut and paste in random order onto the bingo grid (handout 3c).

WASHINGTON, DC

38 Matchups: Government Sites and Symbols

The Capitol Building	is where Congress meets.
The White House	is the President's official home.
The Supreme Court Building	is where the judicial branch meets.
Washington, D.C.	is the capital city of the United States.
The elephant	is a symbol of the Republican party.
The donkey	is a symbol of the Democratic party.
The Great Seal	is used on official U.S. documents.
Uncle Sam	is an imaginary person who symbolizes the government.
The United States flag	is red, white, and blue.
Independence Hall	is where the Constitution was written.
The Liberty Bell	is a symbol of freedom located in Philadelphia.
The Statue of Liberty	is a symbol of freedom and international friendship.

Listening to the News

Directions: Listen to the news. Put an *X* in front of the words each time you hear them.

People

_____ President

_____ Vice President

_____ Governor

_____ Mayor

_____ Congress

Places

_____ Washington, D.C.

_____ the White House

_____ the Capitol

_____ city hall

_____ _____
(state capital)

Topics

_____ crime

_____ taxes

_____ election

_____ community

_____ meeting

All Levels ↑

Intermediate Level ↓

_____ senators

_____ representatives

_____ Republicans

_____ Democrats

_____ the Middle East

_____ Central America

_____ the Soviet Union

_____ China

_____ budget

_____ pollution

_____ trial

_____ debt

Other People:

_____ _____

_____ _____

_____ _____

_____ _____

Other Places:

_____ _____

_____ _____

_____ _____

_____ _____

Other Topics:

_____ _____

_____ _____

_____ _____

_____ _____

Government in the Newspaper

The White House

AP/World Wide

Government in the Newspaper (continued)

National Park Service, courtesy of www.parkphotos.com.

Collection, The Supreme Court Historical Society. Photographed by Richard Strauss, Smithsonian Institute

Government in the Newspaper (continued)

HEADLINES

Inauguration Day

House Now in Session

Visits to White House Increase

Supreme Court Becoming Increasingly Diverse

CAPTIONS

With the First Lady watching, President Clinton is sworn in for his second term by Chief Justice William Rehnquist on January 20, 1997.

Members of the House of Representatives begin a new session today with the swearing-in ceremony.

Record number of tourists are visiting the White House.

Today's Supreme Court is more diverse than any in our nation's history.

Chart: State and Local Leaders

State Government

State _____

Capital _____

Governor _____

Local Government

County _____

City _____

Mayor _____

Personal Information Form

Name	(last)	(first)	(middle)
Number	Street		
City		State	Zip Code
County		Social Security Number	
(Area Code)	Telephone Number		

Matchups: The Civil War

Slaves	were people owned by other people.
The North	was against slavery.
The South	was for slavery.
Factories	were in the North.
Plantations	were large farms with slaves in the South.
Cotton	was grown on plantations in the South.
Dixie	was a name for the South and its flag.
Abraham Lincoln	was the President during the Civil War.
The Emancipation Proclamation	was Lincoln's document to free the slaves.
The Civil War	was from 1861 to 1865.
Ulysses S. Grant	was commander of the Northern army.
Robert E. Lee	was commander of the Southern army.

Abraham Lincoln and the Civil War

Abraham Lincoln was born in Kentucky in 1809.

As a boy, he worked to help his poor family.

So he didn't go to school often, but he loved to read.

When he was twenty-one, he moved to Illinois.

There he was a lawyer and was elected to Congress in 1847.

In 1860, Lincoln was elected the sixteenth President of the United States.

While he was President, the Civil War began.

The North fought the South in the Civil War.

The South wanted to keep slavery.

But Lincoln believed that slavery was wrong.

So he freed the slaves by the Emancipation Proclamation in 1863.

In 1865, the North won the Civil War.

Only one week after the war ended, Lincoln was killed.

A man who loved the South shot him in Washington, D.C.

Today we remember Lincoln as the President who freed the slaves.

Trifold Activity

What do you see in this picture?

Who is this man?

fold here

- -

ABRAHAM LINCOLN:
A GREAT PRESIDENT

Who is Abraham Lincoln?

Why is he important in U.S. history?

fold here

- -

Abraham Lincoln was born in Kentucky on February 12, 1809. When he was 7 years old, his family moved to Indiana. His family was poor. His parents did not go to school, but they knew Abraham wanted to learn. Sometimes teachers came to his town, but he got most of his education by reading books by himself.

When Lincoln was 21, his family moved to Illinois. Here Lincoln had different jobs. He worked in a store and a post office. He became a lawyer and a congressman. In 1861 he became the 16th president of the United States.

Lincoln was president for 4 hard years. This was the time of the Civil War. The northern states were at war with the southern states. The South wanted slavery but the North did not. Lincoln freed the slaves in 1863 with the Emancipation Proclamation. The Civil War ended on April 9, 1865. Five days later, a man from the South killed President Lincoln in Washington, D.C. Americans think that Lincoln was a great president.

Directions: Answer these questions with a partner.

1. How did Abraham Lincoln get his education?

2. What different jobs did he have?

3. When did Lincoln become president?

4. Why did the United States have the Civil War?

5. When was Lincoln born?

6. When and how did he die?

Directions: Write a sentence for each picture.

Abraham Lincoln 1861-1865

_____   _____

_____

Skit: A House Divided

A skit about a Civil War family for ten actors.

Scene 1. Sitting around the table

NARRATOR: It is a small town in Mississippi in the fall of 1862. It is raining outside as the Hill family talks at dinner.

GEORGE HILL (father): *(holding wet cotton)* I'm worried. With so much rain, we won't be able to pick the cotton. We could lose everything.

MARY HILL (mother): You're right. I'm worried too.

TOM HILL (son): Cassie, please bring some more grits and peas! I'm hungry!

CASSIE (slave): Yes, Master Tom.

JEB HILL (son): Why are you hungry? *I'm (points to self)* the one who worked outside today.

TOM: Yeah. You worked real hard giving orders to the slaves without getting *your* hands dirty!

JEB: You forget that *we* own the place. Remember, we are *white*.

TOM: Yes, but how does that make us better than the slaves?

JEB: *(getting angry)* There he goes again, Father. Is he really my brother?

GEORGE: Boys, boys, don't argue. We've had this discussion many times before.

ANN (daughter): This plantation has been in our family for many years.

MARY: It belonged to your grandfather and his father before him.

JEB: Well, my dear brother would gladly give it to the slaves.

TOM: No. But I'd gladly set them free. People are not property. They have human rights.

UNCLE JOHN: Where's your loyalty, my boy? We need good cheap workers for the fields.

GEORGE: Our whole economy depends on slave labor.

MARY: He's right. Listen to your father.

UNCLE JOHN: The government wants to ruin the South. Congress is taxing our imports from Europe.

GEORGE: The North has many factories to produce what it needs. But the South is almost all farmland.

UNCLE JOHN: And now the North doesn't ship us tools and machinery.

ANN: The South is in trouble.

Scene 2. Standing at the door

NARRATOR: It is several months later. One of the Hill family's slaves, Jesse, has run away. He went North to find freedom.

ANN: Mother, why did Jesse run away?

MARY: *(very upset)* It's hard to understand. We treated him so well.

ANN: What will Cassie and the children do without him?

UNCLE JOHN: *(angry)* They'd better not run too. The overseer will catch them.

GEORGE: Many slaves are running north. Soon all of them will run for freedom.

UNCLE JOHN: Abraham Lincoln was no President to us.

GEORGE: His Emancipation Proclamation freed our slaves and destroyed the South.

JEB: Long live *our* president, Jefferson Davis! Long live the Confederate States of America! *(waves Dixie flag)*

Scene 3. Talking at the table

NARRATOR: The Civil war was on land and on sea. The Northern navy tried to stop the South from sending its cotton to other countries. Still the war went on.

JEB: Father, I must join the army. General Robert E. Lee needs strong young men.

GEORGE: Go, Jeb. Fight for our land and our country.

TOM: My body's in the South, but my heart is with the North. I'm joining the Union army.

MARY: Oh, no! *(jumps up)* You can't fight against each other!

GEORGE: Tom, where is your loyalty to our family, to our South?

Skit: A House Divided (continued)

TOM: I must fight for what I believe. I believe slavery is wrong. I'm leaving now! *(gets up and goes out the door)*

CASSIE: Master Tom, be careful!

JIM (slave): The Lord go with you.

NEIGHBOR: *(rushing up)* The overseer caught Jesse. The dogs got him and tore him half to death!

MARY: Our plantation is failing, our slaves are running, our sons are fighting each other. All is lost.

UNCLE JOHN: First our country, now our family.

GEORGE: Lincoln was right when he said, "A house divided against itself cannot stand."

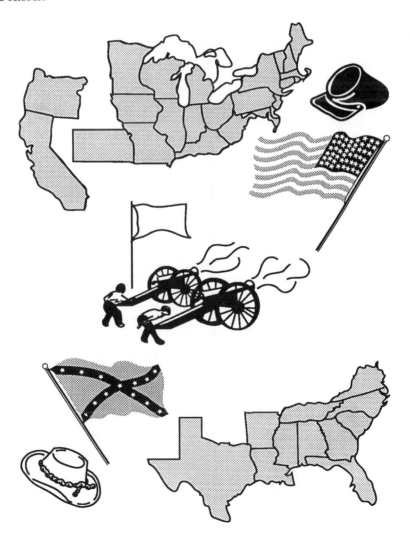

Information Gap: Twentieth-Century Time Line

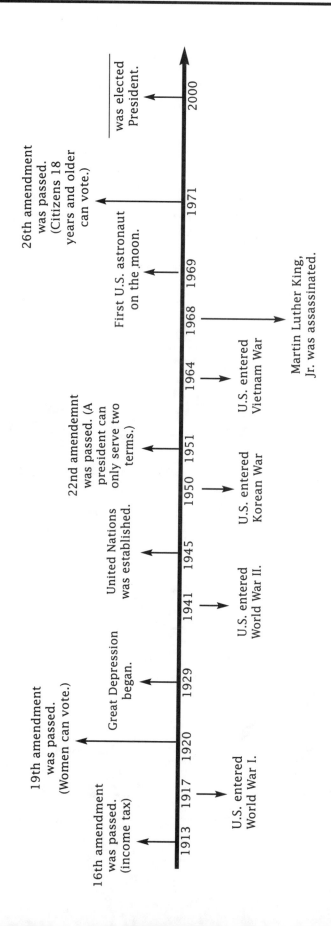

Partner One

Directions: Ask your partner questions to find out the missing information. Write the information on the lines. Do not look at your partner's paper.

Examples: What happened in _____ ?

When did _____ ?

When was _____ ?

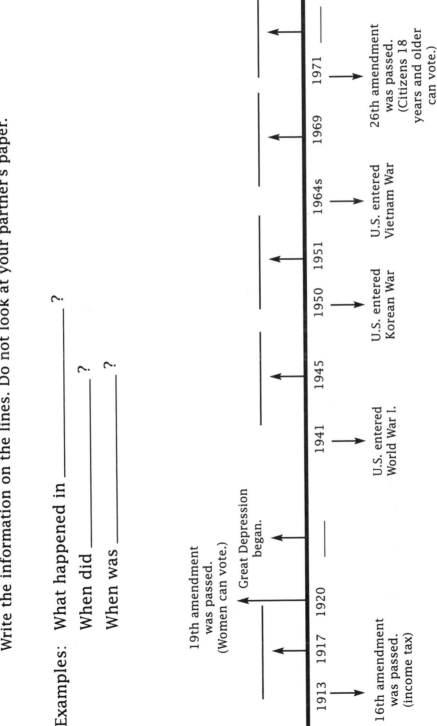

1913   1917   1920

16th amendment was passed. (income tax)

19th amendment was passed. (Women can vote.)

Great Depression began.

1941

U.S. entered World War I.

1945

1950   1951

U.S. entered Korean War

1964s

U.S. entered Vietnam War

1969   1971

26th amendment was passed. (Citizens 18 years and older can vote.)

Partner Two

Directions: Ask your partner questions to find out the missing information.
Write the information on the lines. Do not look at your partner's paper.

Examples: What happened in _____ ?

When did _____ ?

When was _____ ?

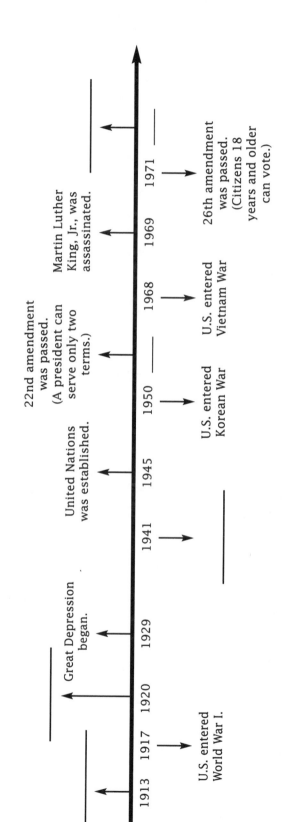

Chart Reading: The U.S. in Conflict—Twentieth Century

War	U.S. Involvement	Taking Sides	Why the U.S. Entered	Results
World War I	1917-1918	The U.S. joins England, Russia, and France *vs.* Germany, Austria-Hungary, and Italy	The U.S. opposed unrestricted submarine warfare by Germany.	England, Russia, France, and the U.S. won. The League of Nations was founded.
World War II	1941-1945	The U.S. joins Allies (England, Russia, France and others) *vs.* Axis Powers (Germany, Italy, and Japan)	Japan attacked the U.S. at Pearl Harbor, Hawaii.	The Allies won. The U.S. and Russia became world powers. The United Nations was founded.
Korean War	1950–1953	The U.S. joins South Korea *vs.* North Korea and China	The U.S. wanted to protect South Korea from Communist invasion from the north.	North Korea and South Korea became two separate countries.
Vietnam war (undeclared)	1964–1973	The U.S. joins South Vietnam and others *vs.* North Vietnam and other Communist countries	The U.S. wanted to prevent Communist aggression against South Vietnam.	The U.S. withdrew. North and South Vietnam were forcibly reunited as the Socialist Republic of Vietnam.

Chart Reading: The U.S. in Conflict–
Twentieth Century (continued)

Directions: Look at the chart. Answer these questions.

1. Which war did the United States enter in 1964? _____

2. Why did the U.S. enter World War I? _____

3. Who won World War II? _____

4. Which countries fought in the Korean War? _____

5. Who attacked the U.S. at Pearl Harbor? _____

6. When did this happen? _____

7. Which countries were enemies of the U.S. during World War II?

   _____

8. Who won World War I? _____

9. After which war was the United Nations formed? _____

10. When was the U.S. involved in the Korean War? _____

Chronological Lineup

Columbus discovered America.

English settlers raised and traded tobacco at Jamestown.

The Pilgrims came to America for religious freedom.

The thirteen colonies began to fight England in the Revolutionary War.

Thomas Jefferson wrote the Declaration of Independence.

The thirteen states decided to write a constitution.

George Washington became the first President of the United States.

During the War of 1812, Francis Scott Key wrote "The Star-Spangled Banner."

Abraham Lincoln freed the slaves.

President Lincoln was killed just after the Civil War ended.

The United States fought in World War I.

The United States fought in World War II.

The United Nations was established.

The United States fought in the Korean War.

The United States fought in the Vietnam war.

_____ was elected President of the United States.

Bingo: Review of Numbers and Dates

Directions: Cut and paste in random order onto the bingo grid (handout 3c).

9	18	2
6	July 4, 1776	26
100	435	3
50	1787	13

Elimination Exercise

Directions: Cross out the word that does not belong.

Example: Independence Day, President's Day, Flag Day, Monday X

1. legislative, municipal, executive, judicial

2. Washington, Lincoln, Jefferson, King

3. Jamestown, Pilgrims, Indians, Thanksgiving

4. red, white, blue, black

5. Congress, lawmakers, senators, justices

6. North, Revolutionary War, South, Lincoln

7. Columbus, Spain, *Mayflower*, New World

8. Senate, President, Vice President, cabinet

9. White House, Capitol, Supreme Court Building, Philadelphia

10. Liberty Bell, flag, Congress, Statue of Liberty

11. Constitution, Bill of Rights, Preamble, Declaration of Independence

12. Representative, 25+ years old, 6-year term, citizen 7+ years

13. justices, Supreme Court, nine, executive

14. Lincoln, Kennedy, King, Franklin

15. speech, assembly, press, voting

16. citizen 9+ years, 35+ years old, 2-term limit, President

```
                      P __ __ __ __ __ __   __ __ __ __ __

     __ __ __ __ A __   __ __ __ __ __ __ __ __ __

          __ __ T __ __   __ __ __ __ __

     __ __ __ R __ __ __   __ __ __ __ __ __

__ __ __ __ __ __ __ __   __ I __ __ __ __ __

          __ __ O __ __ __ __ __ __ __ __ __ __

__ __ __ __ __ __   __ __ T __ __ __   __ __ __ __   __ __

     __ __ __ __ __ __ __ S __ __ __ __   __ __ __
```

Directions: Start at the *top* of the puzzle. Spell out the complete names of these patriots as you work downward. Follow the clues below.

1. Said "Give me liberty or give me death."
2. The main writer of the Declaration of Independence.
3. Made the first United States flag.
4. Led fellow slaves to freedom in the North before the Civil War.
5. Was President during the Civil War.
6. The President called "The Father of Our Country."
7. A twentieth century civil rights leader.
8. The writer of "The Star-Spangled Banner."

----

cut or fold here

Harriet Tubman   Thomas Jefferson

Martin Luther King, Jr.   Abraham Lincoln

Patrick Henry   Francis Scott Key

Betsy Ross   George Washington

Who Am I?

President _____	William Rehnquist
Vice President _____	Thomas Jefferson
First Lady _____	Ulysses S. Grant
Governor _____	Benjamin Franklin
Mayor _____	Patrick Henry
U.S. Senator _____	Robert E. Lee
U.S. Senator _____	Christopher Columbus
U.S. Representative _____	Betsy Ross
George Washington	Harriet Tubman
Abraham Lincoln	Martin Luther King, Jr.
Francis Scott Key	Susan B. Anthony
John F. Kennedy	Sandra Day O'Connor